THE ART OF
CHIP CARVING

THE ART OF
CHIP CARVING

15 GEOMETRIC PATTERNS TO CREATE IN WOOD

TATIANA BALDINA

THE GUILD OF MASTER CRAFTSMAN PUBLICATIONS

— CONTENTS —

INTRODUCTION

Chip carving is perhaps the simplest form of carving, but it can generate a huge variety of intricate and beautiful surface decoration, which can be used to embellish a wide range of objects, from boxes to plates and wall panels to furniture. Whether you are new to chip carving or are already familiar with it, I will show you how to create stunning geometric patterns.

The simplest chips are the base and main component of the patterns: a straight-wall chip, for example, can turn into a large preparatory surface, and a three- or four-sided chip can turn into a multifaceted chip. This makes it possible not only to make the carving more complex, but also to remove unnecessary sharp edges.

When I started out, I spent some time diving into the art of chip carving when what I really wanted was to find a way to use layers in my carving, but

I had no idea what I needed to do or how to make it happen. So in the end I just decided to park this desire in my subconscious brain and continued to carve on. However, a few years later, chip carving led me to one pattern, which rapidly began to develop into exactly what I had dreamed of.

There is a certain excitement before carving a complex pattern – when the drawing has already been completely prepared or transferred on to the surface of the wood and it remains only to take a

knife in your hand – where maximum concentration is required. I have my own method to neutralize this excitement: I conduct a small analysis or 'scan' of a pattern.

In my dictionary there are such concepts as 'weak' and 'strong' chips (elements) in carving. I mentally break any pattern into certain groups of chips connected to each other; I see how the details of carving are connected to each other; I analyse the steps in the carving and which element I should carve first. I usually carve out strong (mostly big) chips first and then work on weak (mainly small or intricate) ones. Regardless, each pattern is unique in its integrity and my rule is subject to change, but not too significantly.

This book consists of 15 small complex patterns that are almost equal in difficulty. The steps show you how to work in one quarter or section at a time, and the templates for the designs can be found on pages 172–3.

For carving, you will need just one skew knife. If you use a skew knife with a standard size and shape specifically for carving such complex patterns, where there are many small and intricate

details, then it's safe to say that you have not one, but two tools in your hands. The first tool is how you handle the knife while carving – for example, whether you can easily undercut curved facets that, in particular, go along the grain; if you know how deep your knife is in the wood at a given moment; and so on – and it will determine whether the second tool in your knife will open up to you or if you will need more practice to make it happen.

This second tool, however strange it may sound, is the tip of a knife. Although it is an inseparable part of the cutting blade, the tip is also a distinct and unique part of the knife, and capable of doing the most delicate carving.

The main thing that inspired me at the beginning of my chip carving journey was a desire to find new forms. Many years have passed, and the complexity of my carving and my perception of it has changed, but I still continue to search. My goal is not just to make simple or complex patterns on wooden pieces; rather, I really want to try and find a balance in every design and work I create.

Welcome to the world of chip carving!

TOOLS AND MATERIALS

You will not need many tools and materials to start chip carving. A good skew knife and the means to keep it sharp are essential, along with drawing materials and a basswood board to carve.

BASSWOOD BOARD

In this book I have used basswood (*Tilia americana*) for all the projects. Also known as linden, this is the first kind of wood that I worked on when I was first learning to carve. This wood is ideal for chip carving, if it is properly dried, because it is relatively soft and light, of a uniform structure and easy to cut.

MECHANICAL PENCIL

To draw the patterns on to the basswood board, I use a 0.5–0.7mm mechanical pencil with an H or HB (#3 or #2) lead. This gives a thin and precise line. I use a polymer eraser for removing pencil lines, as it is neither too soft nor too hard.

COMPASS

You can use any compass as long as it allows you to draw small circles (about 4.5mm in diameter).

RULER

I would suggest using a transparent ruler when ruling lines: the black guidelines on it stand out clearly on a white sheet of paper or on a light wood surface, and I find this helpful when drawing the patterns.

TYPES OF KNIFE

For the small patterns of this book, I recommend a knife that has a blade that is neither too wide nor too narrow with a more or less pronounced tip to carve and undercut relatively large surfaces as well as small details and curved facets.

There are many types of skew knife suitable for chip carving, from standard knife sizes to what we in Russia call knife-hatchets. The blade of the knife, up to the handle, can vary between about 2cm to 4cm in length, starting from the heel and not including the tip of the knife. The size of the blade can also vary.

Skew knives and knife-hatchets can either have a pronounced tip or not. The knife handles can have different shapes and sizes, from narrow to wide and round. I have worked with three brands of knives: Flexcut (I like their KN11 Flexcut skew knife), Forged Tool by Naumov (www.etsy.com/shop/forgedchisel) and Beaver Craft.

Basically, there are no bad knives; you just need to choose the one that is right for you. You may find you like another type of rigid-blade skew knife to carve patterns, as long as it is comfortable to hold and does not tire your hand while carving.

Above *A KN11 Flexcut skew knife.*

Left *A knife-hatchet.*

TECHNIQUES

Here I describe the main techniques you will need to tackle the projects in this book, including sharpening knives, transferring a pattern to the board, and making stop cuts and undercuts.

SAFETY

These are the most basic safety precautions for working with carving knives.

1. Work at a table of comfortable height. There should be no foreign objects on the table, only the necessary tools: board, pencil, compass, eraser and ruler when drawing; board or other wooden blanks and knife when carving.

2. The workplace should be well lit, preferably from all sides. If it is daytime, then daylight should be enough if you sit by a window.

3. Remove the carved-out chips from the carving area as you work as they can cause damage to the edges of the work you have done.

4. Focus only on carving. For example, carve for 20–30 minutes, then take a break for 10 minutes to rest your hands and eyes. When you are tired and find it difficult to focus only on carving, your chances of cutting yourself or breaking the carving are higher.

5. Work only with a sharp knife. Remember that you can cut yourself either by not adhering to the safety precautions, not using your supporting hand when carving or when working with a dull knife.

6. Your supporting hand should not be in the way of the knife's movement and, in general, should be well away from the carving process. While working with a skew knife, the supporting hand both holds the board and participates in carving.

The supporting hand should be kept away from the direction of the knife's movement while carving to avoid cutting yourself.

SHARPENING A KNIFE

Get into the habit of sharpening your knife regularly, especially before you start work on a new pattern (or a part of a pattern that requires very sharp multi-level patterns), as this will help to give you consistent results.

My preferred sharpening method is to use abrasive or sandpaper films or strips. I stick these along the edge of a sheet of glass that has had the sharp edge removed **❶**. The sandpaper films I use range from 600 or 2000 to 6000 grit. The very first sandpaper I use depends on the condition of my knife at the moment I am going to sharpen it. The highest grit I use instead of a leather strip; I use this for polishing. The lower the grit of a film, the fewer movements you make when sharpening; the higher its grit, the more movements you make. You make roughly three or four knife movements on each side of the knife when sharpening on 2000 grit; five or six movements on 3000 grit; and seven or eight movements on 6000 grit.

For me, skew blades are best sharpened while oriented to run in a straight line ❷. In my opinion, this works best because it is easier to hold at a constant angle, and leads to a more highly polished cutting surface before using higher-grit sandpaper and polishing. Sharpening along the surface of the films tends to result in a rounded cutting edge,

even if I try to hold a constant angle ❸. A strip of leather (also known as a strop) can be used along with some honing paste to polish the surface of the bevel.

After sharpening the blade, rinse it with water and wipe dry. And after you have finished working with the knife, wipe it gently (so as not to cut yourself) with a dry rag. Put a block of solid foam on the cutting edge to protect it ❹ and wrap the tool in a case roll or store it in a special box ❺.

❶ Abrasive strips stuck on to a sheet of glass.

❷ This shows the best method I have found to sharpen a straight-edge skewed blade using abrasive films.

❸ This shows how you can sharpen a knife along the surface of the films; however, every time I use this method I obtain a rounded cutting edge even if I try to hold a constant angle.

❹ Solid foam on the cutting edge protects the blade.

❺ Keep the knife in a special box for tools.

TRANSFERRING THE PATTERN TO THE BASSWOOD BOARD

Before you can start drawing the patterns, you need to prepare the basswood board. If you are a beginner, I would advise you to transfer the patterns with carbon paper (the templates for the designs in this book can be found on pages 172–3). If you already have some experience, you can draw the patterns by hand, following the steps described for each project in this book.

To transfer a pattern, first scan or photocopy the relevant template from the book. Print out the pattern if you have scanned it.

Next, lay the carbon paper, ink-coated side down, on to the board where the pattern should go ❶. Place the printed pattern on top of the carbon paper, then fasten these sheets to the board with masking tape so that they do not move ❷.

Trace over the pattern using an HB pencil (a standard one, not a mechanical one) or a ball-point pen that has run out of ink. Be sure to press hard enough with the pencil or pen to transfer the design on to the wood through the layers of paper ❸. When you are sure that all the details have been transferred, remove the tape and sheets ❹.

❶ The carbon paper in place on the wood, ink side down.

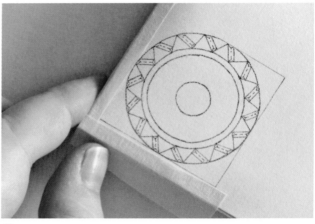
❷ Fasten the sheets to the board with masking tape.

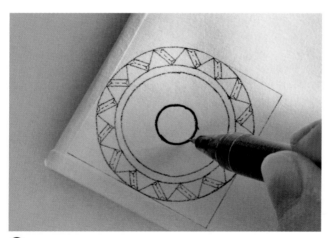
❸ Here I used a ball-point pen that has run out of ink to transfer the design on to the wood.

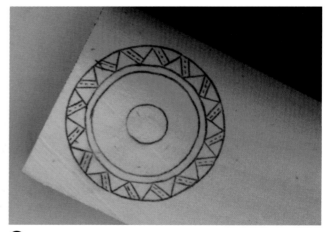
❹ Remove the tape and sheets when all of the design has been transferred.

HOLDING A SKEW KNIFE

When carving, there are two directions of movement of a skew knife – towards yourself and away from yourself. The carving motion of the knife towards yourself is when the heel of the knife is turned towards you ❶. The carving motion of the knife away from yourself is when the heel of the knife is turned away from you ❷.

❶ The heel of the knife turned towards you.

❷ The heel of the knife turned away from you.

STOP CUTS

Stop cuts are the cuts made in the places where the facets of the chips connect with each other, starting from the deepest part of the chip. When you take the first steps in carving and practise carving simple patterns again and again, stop cuts not only show you where to stop undercutting one side or the other of any chip, but also set the depth of the chip (I talk more about this and practise undercuts on triangles; see page 22).

Before you start to carve you need to make stop cuts, not only to feel the angle at which the knife tilts when undercutting the chips – triangles, ovals and

so on – but so you do not go beyond the previously made stop cuts first. You also need to be aware of 'invisible' stop cuts: the angle at which the knife tilts when undercutting these chips is different; therefore, it takes some time for the muscle memory to remember these tilts and the angle of undercutting.

Stop cuts are made perpendicular to the surface of the wood, starting from the deepest point of the chip. Place the knife where the deepest point will be ❶. Push the knife deep into the wood ❷, then lower the heel to the base ❸. These steps are then repeated on the other stop cut lines.

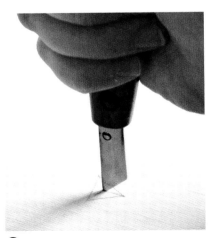

❶ Knife set at the deepest point.

❷ Push the knife deep into the wood.

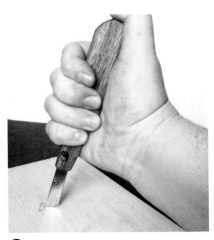

❸ Lower the heel to the base.

UNDERCUTTING

Undercutting refers to the repetitive motion of a knife at one angle on all sides of any chip in order to completely remove it.

To make an undercut, hold the knife with four fingers at a comfortable distance from the knife blade. Let your thumb lie on the knife handle. Set the undercutting angle at 45 degrees. In the picture, I demonstrate the undercutting technique using the example of a triangle. Hold the board with your second hand, and put the thumb of your supporting hand on the back edge of the blade to push the knife ❶.

Now undercut the second side of a triangle, but this time working away from you ❷. This grip is more complicated to master than the first one. At the top of the handle, place the thumb, forefinger and middle finger, with the thumb and forefinger together and the middle finger a bit further away, closer to the blade of the knife ❸. At the bottom of the handle, the ring finger supports the knife ❹ and the little finger is at a comfortable distance from the carved pattern ❺. This can regulate the angle at which the knife is tilted in relation to the carved pattern ❻. In this image I am undercutting the base of a triangle by cutting towards myself ❼.

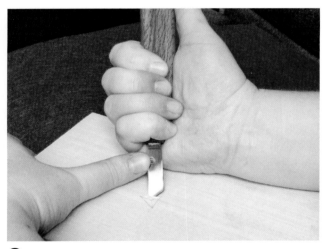

❶ Holding the board with the second hand, and pushing the knife on the back edge with the thumb.

❷ Undercutting the second side of a triangle in the position away from you.

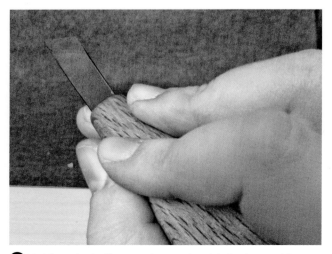

❸ Holding the knife to undercut the side in the position away from you – view from above.

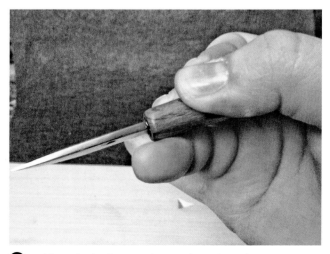

❹ Holding the knife to undercut the side in the position away from you – position of the ring finger.

5 Undercutting the side away from you – little finger held out of the way.

6 Regulating the angle at which the knife is tilted.

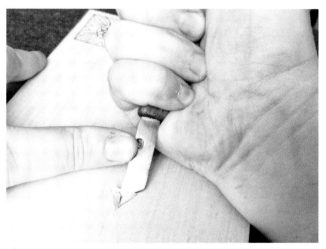

7 Undercutting the base of a triangle towards yourself.

Many woodcarvers say that it is necessary to grind the surface of the wood before you start carving. I do not agree, since the knife will become dull much faster than if the surface of the wood is not polished before carving.

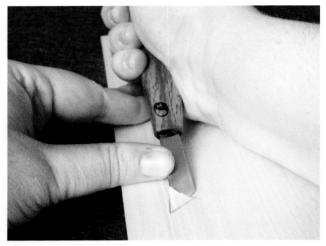

1 Undercutting where the sides are not clearly along or against the grain.

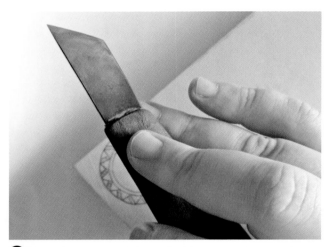

2 To undercut a straight-wall chip, use your second hand to steady the knife.

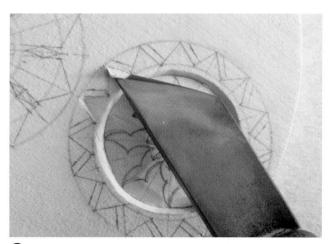

3 Undercutting a straight-wall chip away from you.

STRAIGHT-WALL CHIPS

A straight-wall chip is the simplest pattern in chip carving. It can be either an equilateral triangle (where all three sides are equal) or an isosceles triangle (where two of the sides are equal). No stop cuts are needed to carve this. Accordingly, there is no need to keep the knife at the same angle while undercutting the sides in a simple triangle to remove the chip, which has three facets, or when a triangle is divided into three parts or three straight-wall chips.

Undercutting a straight-wall chip towards yourself
To undercut a straight-wall chip towards yourself, when the sides are not clearly located along the grain or against the grain, you need to undercut very carefully. To do this, when the sides are undercut at an angle of almost 90 degrees, hold the knife in your hand, away from the blade, so that the blade is laid as close as possible to the surface of the wood. Next, hold the board with the free fingers of your second hand and place the thumb of this supporting hand on the knife's back edge. This will act as a kind of counterweight: the hand with the knife moves forwards and slightly to the left, as if grabbing the side along which the tip moves and, accordingly, inside the wood if there is no counterweight. Instead we need the knife to move parallel to the side to which it is going 1.

Undercutting a straight-wall chip away from yourself
The last technique involves undercutting a straight-wall chip away from yourself. If you try to cut it like a triangle, by moving away from you, you will not be able to lay the knife blade close to the surface of the wood. Hold your fingers away from the blade. The thumb and forefinger should be together, the middle finger a little further from them and closer to the blade of the knife, and the ring finger will be next to the little finger 2. In this case, it will be possible to put the knife blade on the surface of the wood and carve the chip 3.

*An angle of almost
60 degrees.*

*An angle of almost
90 degrees.*

that tone of oil go deep into the grain. Before adding the next layer of oil, brush the carved surface with a clean soft toothbrush. I do not like using sandpaper, because one of the most important aspects in chip carving is to keep the edges of the carving sharp.

Second layer: Apply a layer of Danish oil with a stain. Third layer: Apply another layer of Danish oil with a stain. Fourth layer: Apply a layer of Danish oil without any stain.

CARVING AT DIFFERENT ANGLES

Carving of all chips can be done at any angle you want. However, there are some basic angles for undercutting, when this or that chip looks best on the surface of the wood:

For undercutting two sides of a straight-wall chip, you need to make a cut at an angle of almost 90 degrees to the surface of the wood.

MULTI-LEVEL CARVING

In the instructions for the patterns, I sometimes refer to multi-level carving. This is a type of carving when smaller straight-wall chips are carved inside larger straight-wall chips. These smaller and larger chips can be in the form of isosceles triangles but also other forms and shapes too.

FINISHING

Rather than hiding the work you have done with thick layers of stain and varnish, finishing should reveal the carving and enhance its beauty, which is what Danish oil does. You can buy Danish oil with or without an added stain. It can be applied both with a synthetic brush (when applying oil on carving) or with a soft rag (when applying oil to a smooth wood surface).

First layer: Apply a clear Danish oil without any stain. This layer of oil prepares the wood grain and carved surface for the next layers of oil with any kind of tone (light or dark ones) and does not let

A piece finished with Danish oil.

You do not have to use Danish oil mixed with a stain straight from the jar or tin. If you do not find a shade that you like, you can mix Dainish oil with different stains together in a ratio of your choice. Use a scrap of wood to practise on before applying it to your finished piece.

THE PATTERNS

Pattern 1

BLOOMING

The first pattern consists of multi-level straight-wall chips and six-sided chips, which are connected to two-sided chips.

TOOLS AND MATERIALS

- Basswood board (at least 100mm square, 1.5mm thick)

- 5mm mechanical pencil with H or HB (#3 or #2) lead

- Ruler

- Compass

- Skew knife

- Sandpaper or leather strips for sharpening

DRAWING PROCESS

First prepare a main circle for the pattern. Using a compass, draw a circle with a radius of 2cm. Then draw two perpendicular lines that intersect at the centre and two diagonal lines that divide the quarters of the circle in half, forming eighths. Now divide the spaces in half again, so you have a circle with 16 identical triangles. Using a pencil and starting from the top of one of the perpendicular lines, mark each of the lines clockwise with numbers: 1, 2, 3. . .16. These marks will help when you are drawing the main pattern.

Practise undercuts on triangles

When just starting to carve or if you have yet to develop enough muscle memory, one challenge in chip carving is to understand where the knife tip currently is and how deeply to undercut a facet. Sometimes, usually at the initial stages, you think you did not push the tip of the knife deep enough into the wood and you have to do so a little deeper. In this case, I suggest that, before carving any pattern of this book or any other complex patterns, you experiment. Start by drawing several triangles of different sizes, then make stop cuts inside each of them and start to undercut the facets a little, one by one, until they pop out. When carving chips of a normal size you will discover that there is no need to put so much pressure on the knife to push it deep into the wood and completely remove one facet. The 'glow' patterns in this book contain small and intricate details, where you need to work only with the tip of the knife, so this experiment might help you in carving such patterns.

1 Mark two dots 1.4cm and 1.1cm from the centre.

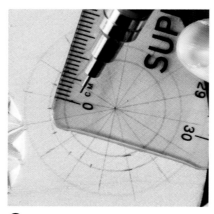

2 Divide the space inside the triangles and mark a dot on the second, larger circle.

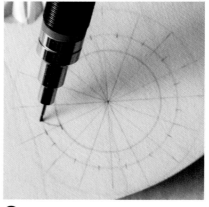

3 Connect the base of the future triangle with the dot on the second circle with a slightly curved line.

Mark two dots on any of the 16 lines: make the first one 1.4cm from the centre of the pattern; the second, 1.1cm from the centre of the pattern **1**. Draw two circles starting at these dots using a compass. Then divide all 16 spaces in half and mark dots on the second, larger circle **2**.

Next, start drawing the main elements of the pattern. To do this, connect the point where the first circle intersects the sides of the triangles with the previously prepared dot on the second circle. Draw a slightly curved line **3**, and then connect the resulting line to the tip of the line at the top of the main circle with an additional straight line **4**.

4 Connect the dot on the second circle with the tip of the line at the main circle.

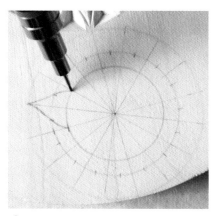

5 Draw a straight line connecting the tip of the line with the dot on the second circle and then a curved line to the base of the triangle.

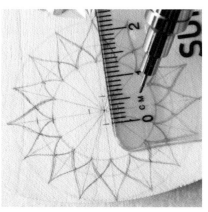

6 Mark a dot 3mm from the centre of the pattern on each of the perpendicular lines.

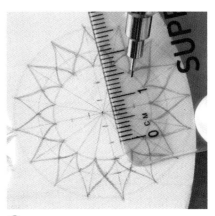

7 Mark a dot 7mm from the centre of the pattern on each of the perpendicular lines.

8 Draw a curved line from the dot on line 1 (7mm) to the dot on line 13 (3mm).

Repeat these steps in reverse order to make a sort of triangle **5**, and then repeat all the steps with the remaining triangles, starting from the centre of the base of the first triangle.

For the interior section of the pattern, mark two dots on each of the perpendicular lines: mark the first dot 3mm from the centre **6**; the second one, 7mm from the centre **7**. As the movement of the lines in the central pattern goes

anticlockwise, start connecting the dots from line 1: draw a curved line from the dot on line 1 (7mm) to the dot on line 13 (3mm), following the contours of the triangles that go along the perimeter of the pattern **8**.

9 Connect the dot where the first circle intersects line 16 with the dot on line 13 (3mm) with a curved line.

10 Connect the dot where the first circle intersects line 15 with the dot on line 13 (3mm) with a curved line.

11 Connect the dot where the first circle intersects line 14 with the dot on line 13 (3mm) with a curved line.

12 The pattern is drawn.

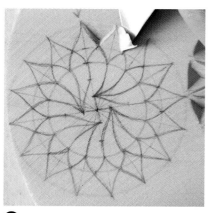

13 Start carving the straight-wall chips that go around the perimeter of the pattern.

14 Draw the lines parallel to the sides of the rhombuses.

Repeat by drawing the following curved lines: connect the dot on line 13 (3mm) where the first circle intersects line 16, where the first circle intersects line 15, and where the first circle intersects line 14, all with the same dot and drawing a curved line **9**, **10**, **11**.

Now repeat these steps in the remaining three quarters of the pattern, starting at one of the perpendicular lines. When all four quarters are filled in, the pattern is ready for carving **12**.

CARVING PROCESS
Begin to carve the pattern with straight-wall chips that go along the perimeter of the pattern **13**. Once they have been cut, draw lines parallel to the sides of the rhombuses, on the left and right of it. Start with one that is on any perpendicular line (on lines 1, 5, 9 or 13). Draw the parallel lines for every other rhombus – that is, the rhombuses that go on lines 1, 3, 5 and so on **14**.

15 Carve the smaller straight-wall chips inside the larger ones.

16 Cut the base of the six-sided chip at an angle of 60 degrees.

17 Undercut the next short side of the six-sided chip.

18 Carve the long facet of the six-sided chip.

19 Change the knife grip in your hand and undercut the shot side.

20 Change the knife in your hand one more time and carve the last short side in the six-sided chip.

Cut the resulting straight-wall chips **15**.

Next, begin to carve the central six-sided chips of the pattern. Start with the one that goes along the grain, as it will then be easier to carve and remove a two-sided chip that is next to it when you are finishing carving the pattern. Undercut the short side or base of the chip at an angle of about 60 degrees **16**,

then, if necessary (depending on how smoothly the knife goes through the wood grain), change the knife grip in your hand and cut the next short side **17**. Change the grip of the knife in your hand again (or leave it unchanged if the previous direction of the knife was away from you) and cut one of the long sides **18**. Turn the knife and carve the next side **19**, then the last short one **20**.

21 Carve the remaining long side of the six-sided chip.

22 Finish carving one of the quarters of the central pattern with the chip that goes along the grain.

23 One of the interior quarters of the central pattern is complete.

24 Divide the outer sides of the rhombuses and draw lines that connect to the base of the rhombuses.

25 Make a cut at an angle of about 90 degrees.

Finally, undercut the remaining long facet **21**. Repeat these steps on each of the long six-sided chips.

In one of the quarters, carve the chips that are between two of the six-sided chips: start with the sides that go against the grain and finish with those chips that go along the grain **22**, **23**.

Next, prepare the rhombuses for carving. To do this, draw two lines inside the first rhombus: divide the outer sides in half by eye or using a ruler and draw lines to these points **24**.

The cuts will go anticlockwise, so set the tip of the knife at the first line, closer to the long central chip, and cut it at an angle of about 90 degrees **25**.

26 Place the knife close to the wood surface and undercut a chip.

27 Cut the place between the rhombuses with a tip of the knife.

28 Place the knife close to the wood surface and undercut the remaining chip in the rhombus.

29 The first rhombus has been carved (see bottom right section).

30 The carving is now complete.

Then lay the knife close to the surface of the wood, as for carving the base of a straight-wall chip, and cut the chip **26**.

Repeat with the remaining lines in the rhombus. To cut the last chip in the rhombus, touch the point between the rhombuses with the tip of the knife **27** and cut it in the same way as for the previous lines, following the grain direction **28**.

Once the first rhombus has been carved **29**, repeat the steps of the carving on the remaining rhombuses in the quarter, then repeat these steps in the three remaining quarters.

The carving is now complete **30**.

WAVE

This pattern consists of a slightly more complicated standard 'glow' and long two-sided chips surrounding the central pattern. When carving rounded chips with outer sides going along the grain, you will discover a technique that will lead to a smooth facet surface.

TOOLS AND MATERIALS

- Basswood board (at least 100mm square, 1.5mm thick)

- 5mm mechanical pencil with H or HB (#3 or #2) lead

- Ruler

- Compass

- Skew knife

- Sandpaper or leather strips for sharpening

1 Mark a dot 5.5mm from the centre of the pattern on line 5.

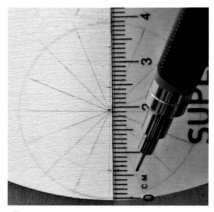

2 Mark another dot 6mm from the main circle of the pattern on line 13.

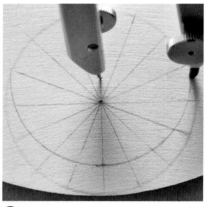

3 Place a compass on the dot on line 5 and draw a curved line with a radius equal to the distance between this dot and the one on line 13.

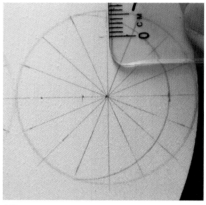

4 Mark a short line 6mm from the main circle on line 9.

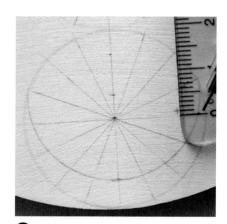

5 Mark a dot on the short line 1mm from line 9.

6 Mark a dot 6mm from the main circle of the pattern on line 1.

DRAWING PROCESS

First prepare a main circle for the pattern. Using a compass, draw a circle with a radius of 2cm. Then draw two perpendicular lines that intersect at the centre and two diagonal lines that divide the quarters of the circle in half, forming eighths. Now divide the spaces in half again, so you have a circle with 16 identical triangles. Using a pencil and starting from the top of one of the perpendicular lines, mark each of the lines clockwise with numbers: 1, 2, 3. . .16. These marks will help when you are drawing the main pattern.

Make the first curved line by first marking two dots: mark the first dot 5.5mm from the centre of the pattern on line 5 **1**; mark the second one 6mm from the main circle of the pattern on line 13 **2**. Place a compass on the dot on line 5 and draw a curved line with a radius equal to the distance between these two dots **3**.

Now mark the next two dots for the second curved line. Make the first dot by marking a short line 6mm from the main circle of the pattern on line 9 **4**; then mark a dot on this shot line 1mm from line 9 **5**. To make the second dot, mark 6mm from the main circle of the pattern on line 1 **6**.

Place a compass on the first dot and draw a curved line with a radius equal to the distance between the two dots **7**.

Next, mark two dots for the third curved line: make one dot 6mm from the main circle of the pattern on line 4 **8**. Place a compass on top of line 12 and draw a curved line with a radius equal to the distance between the dot and the point on line 12 **9**.

Next, mark two dots for the fourth curved line: first, divide the space on the main circle of the pattern between lines 14 and 15 **10** and make a dot; second, mark a dot 5mm from the main circle of the pattern on line 7 **11**.

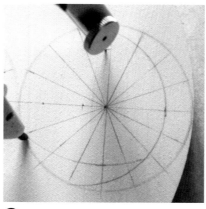

7 Place a compass on the dot on line 9 and draw a curved line with a radius equal to the distance between this dot and the one on line 1.

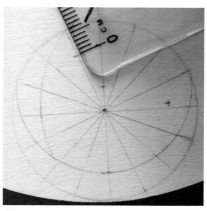

8 Mark a dot 6mm from the main circle of the pattern on line 4.

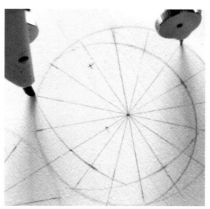

9 Place a compass on the top of line 12 and draw a curved line with a radius equal to the distance between this point and the dot on line 4.

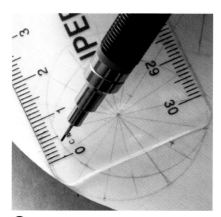

10 Divide the space on the main circle of the pattern between lines 14 and 15 to make the first dot.

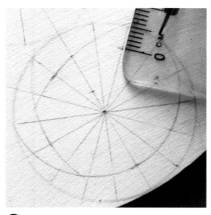

11 Mark a dot 5mm from the main circle of the pattern on line 7.

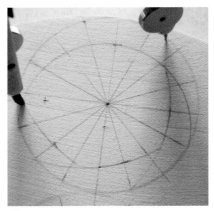

12 Place a compass on the first dot and draw a curved line with a radius equal to the distance between this dot and the one on line 7.

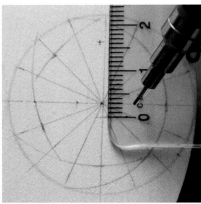

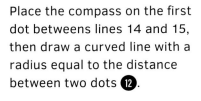

13 Mark a dot 3mm from the centre of the pattern on line 1.

Place the compass on the first dot betweens lines 14 and 15, then draw a curved line with a radius equal to the distance between two dots **12**.

Next, mark two dots for the final curved line: mark the first dot 3mm from the centre of the pattern on line 1 **13**; the second one, 6mm from the main circle of the pattern on line 9 **14**. Place a compass on the first dot and draw a curved line with a radius equal to the distance between two dots **15**.

Measure a radius of 4.5mm from the centre of the pattern **16** and, using a compass, draw a circle.

Mark a dot 1.1cm from the centre of the pattern on line 16 **17** and, using a compass, mark this dot on every other line **18**. Next, connect the dot where one of the curved lines intersects line 1 with the dot on line 16; the dot where one of the curved lines intersects line 15 with a dot on line 14; and so on **19**. The pattern is now ready for carving.

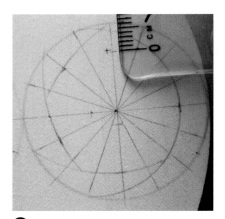

14 Mark a dot 6mm from the main circle of the pattern on line 9.

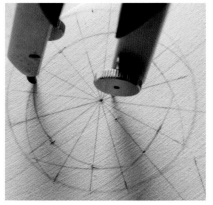

15 Place a compass on the dot on line 1 and draw a curved line with a radius equal to the distance between this dot and the one on line 9.

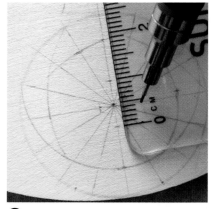

16 Measure a radius of 4.5mm from the centre of the pattern and draw a circle.

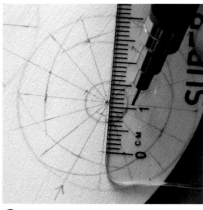

17 Mark a dot 1.1cm from the centre of the pattern on line 16.

CARVING PROCESS

Begin to carve the pattern in the central circle. Carve every other small triangle, starting with the one between lines 16 and 1 **20**.

Cut the sides of the straight-wall chips along the perimeter of the central pattern **21** and carve them **22**.

Make a cut on line 16 **23**, starting from the top of the central small triangle to the top of the straight-wall chip, then repeat on lines 14 and so on.

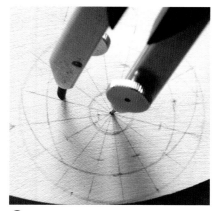

18 Using a compass, mark dots on every other line.

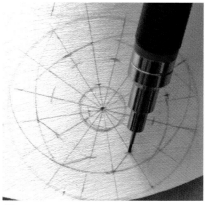

19 Where the lines of the large two-sided chips intersect additional lines, connect the dots with the ones next to them anticlockwise.

20 Carve every other triangle inside the central circle.

21 Cut the sides of the straight-wall chips along the perimeter of the central pattern.

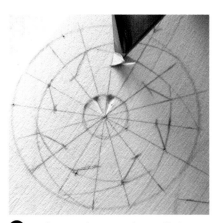

22 Undercut the straight-wall chip.

23 Make a cut on line 16.

24 Lay the knife close to the surface of the wood and make an undercut.

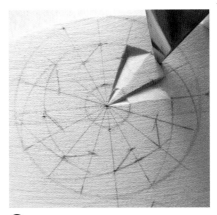

25 Undercut the base of the triangle at an angle of about 45 degrees.

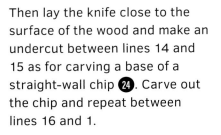

Then lay the knife close to the surface of the wood and make an undercut between lines 14 and 15 as for carving a base of a straight-wall chip **24**. Carve out the chip and repeat between lines 16 and 1.

Undercut the base of the triangle between lines 16 and 15 at an angle of 45 degrees **25**, and then carve the sides of the triangle at an angle of 45 degrees **26**.

Next, draw a line inside the chip between lines 1 and 16: draw it from the top left corner of the chip to the opposite side of the chip where it meets at the circle, or 4.5mm from the centre of the pattern **27**.

Make a cut at an angle of about 90 degrees on the resulting drawn line **28**, then make one more cut at the top of the chip where the facets connect with each other **29**.

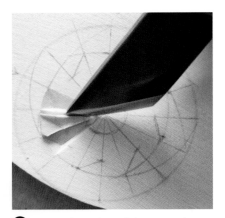

26 Carve the sides of the triangle at an angle of 45 degrees.

27 Draw a line in every other chip from the top left corner of the chip to the opposite side of the chip, where it meets the circle, 4.5mm from the centre of the pattern.

28 Make a cut at an angle of about 90 degrees on the line drawn inside the chip.

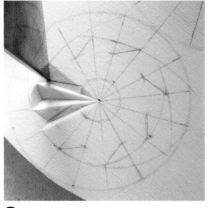

29 Make a cut at the top of the chip where the two facets connect with each other.

Undercut the chip as for carving a base of a straight-wall chip 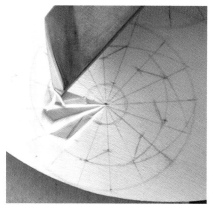. Repeat between lines 14 and 15. One of the sections has been carved 31.

Continue working in the same way with the remaining sections in the central pattern.

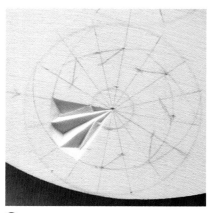

30 Lay the knife down to the wood and undercut the chip as for carving a base of a straight-wall chip.

31 One section of the pattern has been carved.

Find an invisible 'point'

Curved facets that go straight along the grain are simple in appearance but difficult in practice, where the challenge is to undercut the side to get a smooth surface without sharp creases from the straight blade of a knife.

Carving of such sides has always literally caused me fear. But in all types of woodcarving, fear is the driving force. If you do not try to carve what you consider difficult, then there will be no development in what you do. Now I'm not afraid anymore, because I have looked into the eyes of fear called 'carving of the curved side that goes along the grain'.

The technique that I described for the first pattern is partially applicable in carving such facets. Knowing the placement of the tip of the knife is very important in finding an 'invisible point' while making a curved facet. But my technique for undercutting curved sides along the grain is mostly based on imagination and, of course, practice.

Imagine in your head (or draw on paper or on the wood surface) a curved facet. Then imagine or draw a straight line that divides this side into two chips. These two curved chips go along the grain, and when undercutting one chip is in the direction towards yourself and the other chip is in the direction away from you. If you carve these two chips in one go so there is no chipping, the chips will end up with two straight bases. Accordingly, a triangle will be formed in the centre of the entire chip, where the base is in the place where the sides of a two-sided chip are connected to each other. That triangle is an invisible point that needs to be levelled to have a smooth surface as a result.

Of course, you do not need to divide the entire facet in half and carve two chips: it was said figuratively, so that you imagine this place on the facet that needs to be rounded off with curved undercuts and know how you need to direct the knife along the surface of the side.

When you practise carving a curved facet along the grain, it is necessary to feel the knife in your hand and how it moves through the wood grain, and to make 'curved' movements of the knife in the direction away from you and towards yourself from the base to the top of a facet.

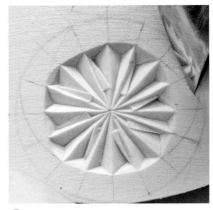

32 Undercut the sides of the first two-sided chip that is at the base of the pattern at an angle of 60–65 degrees.

33 Undercut the base of the first two-sided chip, also at an angle of 60–65 degrees.

Begin to carve the large two-sided chips that go around the central pattern. Start with the sides of a chip that is at the base of the pattern. Undercut two sides at an angle of 60–65 degrees **32**. Then undercut the long side, or base, of the chip **33**.

Start carving the second two-sided chip from the side that connects with the central pattern **34**, then turn the board and, trying not to remove the knife from the wood, cut one facet **35**. Then pull the knife about 1mm out from the wood, without removing the tip of the knife from the wood **36**.

34 Carve the long side of the second two-sided chip that connects with the central pattern.

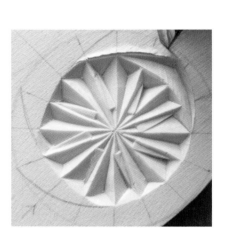

35 Undercut the first outer facet of the second chip.

36 Pull the kife about 1mm out of the wood, without removing the knife.

Undercut the second facet and finish carving the second two-sided chip 37.

Repeat the steps for carving the third two-sided chip, starting from the long side that connects to the central pattern from the most curved place 38. Then undercut the second facet following the grain direction 39. Finally, carve the remaining fourth large chip that goes around the central pattern.

The carving is now complete 40.

37 Finish carving the second two-sided chip.

38 Start carving the third two-sided chip from the line that connects with the central pattern.

39 Finish carving the third two-sided chip before repeating the steps to carve the fourth two-sided chip.

40 The carving is now complete.

KITE

In this pattern, there are simple five-sided chips, which are connected to each other, as well as multi-level chips, where the next undercutting is not parallel to the previous one.

TOOLS AND MATERIALS

- Basswood board (at least 100mm square, 1.5mm thick)

- 5mm mechanical pencil with H or HB (#3 or #2) lead

- Ruler

- Compass

- Skew knife

- Sandpaper or leather strips for sharpening

1 Measure a radius of 9mm from the centre of the pattern and draw a circle.

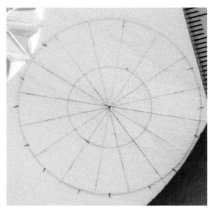

2 Starting from line 1 on the main outside circle, mark a dot 4.5mm to the left and right of every other line.

3 Connect the resulting dots at the point where the interior circle intersects the lines.

4 Measuring from the centre, mark a dot 1.5cm on the line inside each triangle.

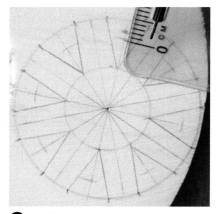

5 Mark a dot 2mm above the first dot on the lines in each triangle.

DRAWING PROCESS

First prepare a main circle for the pattern. Using a compass, draw a circle with a radius of 2cm. Then draw two perpendicular lines that intersect at the centre and two diagonal lines that divide the quarters of the circle in half, forming eighths. Now divide the spaces in half again, so you have a circle with 16 identical triangles. Using a pencil and starting from the top of one of the perpendicular lines, mark each of the lines clockwise with numbers: 1, 2, 3. . .16. These marks will help when you are drawing the main pattern.

Measure a radius of 9mm from the centre on any line in the circle and, using a compass, draw a circle **1**. Mark a dot on the main outside circle of the pattern that is 4.5mm to the left and right of line 1, and then of every odd-number line **2**. Connect the resulting dots with the point where the interior circle intersects the odd-number lines **3**.

Measure a radius of 1.5cm and, using a compass, mark dots on the line inside each triangle **4**. Mark a dot 2mm above the previous dots **5**.

Next, measure a radius of 1.4cm from the centre and, using a compass, mark a dot on the lines in the spaces adjacent to the triangles **6**.

Without changing the radius, mark these dots on the sides of the triangles **7**. Next, measure a radius of 1.7cm and, using a compass, mark dots on the sides of the triangles **8**.

Begin to connect the resulting dots. Draw a curved line by hand, starting from the point where the interior circle intersects the line centred in a space next to a triangle. Draw the curve through the lowest dot on the side of the triangle **9** to the dot on the central line in the triangle. Repeat in the reverse order, continuing the curved line through the lowest dot on the other side of the triangle to the point where the line in the space on the other side of the triangle intersects with the interior circle **10**.

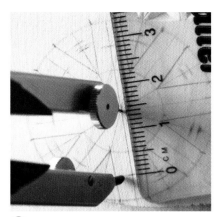

6 Mark a dot 1.4cm on the lines inside the spaces adjacent to the triangles.

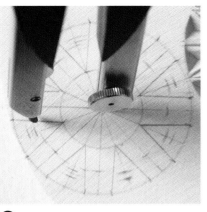

7 Using a compass, also with a radius of 1.4cm, mark dots on the sides of the triangles.

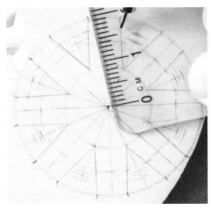

8 Measure a radius of 1.7cm and, using a compass, mark dots on the sides of the triangles.

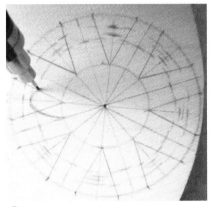

9 Starting where the interior circle intersects a line centred in a space next to a triangle, draw a curved line through the first dot on the side of the triangle to the dot on the central line in the triangle.

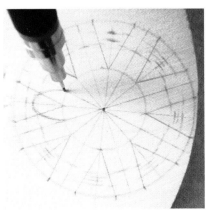

10 Continue to draw the remaining part of the curved line by hand.

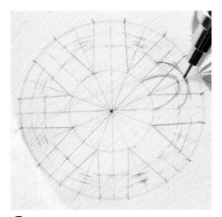

11 Draw a second curve, starting on the line next to the triangle on one side and finishing on the dot on the line on the other side, going through the three dots in or on the triangle.

12 Mark two dots 6mm and 3mm from the centre of the pattern on any line.

13 Connect the points where the second central circle intersects even lines with the points where the first central circle intersects odd lines.

Now make a second curved line above it, starting at the dot on the line next to the triangle and connecting with the second dot on the side of the triangle, the second dot on the central line of the triangle, the second dot on the other side of the triangle and the dot on the line on the other side of the triangle **11**. Repeat these steps with the remaining dots to continue the two curved lines going completely around the pattern.

To make two circles, measure and make a mark on any line 6mm from the centre of the pattern and a second mark 3mm from the centre of the pattern **12**. Using a compass, use these two marks to draw two circles.

Connect the point where the second central circle intersects line 16 with the point where the smaller first central circle intersects with line 1. Then connect the point where the smaller first central circle intersects line 1 with the point where the second circle intersects line 2. Repeat these steps with the remaining points between the two circles **13**. The pattern is now ready for carving.

CARVING PROCESS

Begin to carve the pattern from the central five-sided chips, which are connected to each other by one of the facets. First, undercut the top of the chip at an angle of about 60 degrees **14**, then, without removing the knife from the wood, if possible, undercut the next long side **15**. Change the grip of the knife in your hand and cut the short side **16**. Turn the board and cut the next facet of the chip **17**, and then, also without removing the knife from the wood, if the knife goes smoothly through the wood grain, finish cutting the chip **18**.

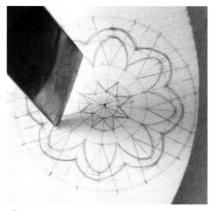

14 Undercut the top of the five-sided chip at an angle of about 60 degrees.

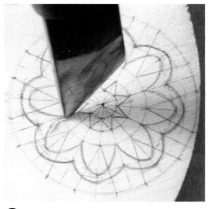

15 Without removing the tip of the knife from the wood, undercut the long facet.

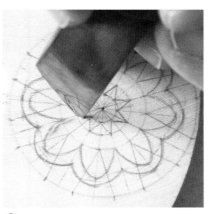

16 Change the knife in your hand and undercut the short side.

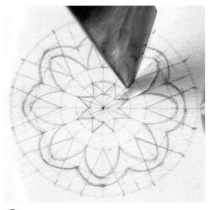

17 Turn the board and start cutting the long side.

18 Without removing the tip of the knife from the wood, undercut the last facet of the chip.

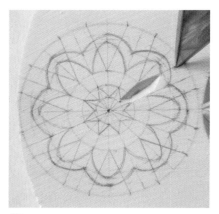

19 Start carving the first four-sided chip above the five-sided chip.

20 Undercut all the sides of the four-sided chip at an angle of 60–65 degrees.

Start carving the four-sided chip, which is like a continuation of the previous five-sided chip, at an angle of about 60 degrees **19**.

Undercut all the sides of the four-sided chip at an angle of 60–65 degrees **20**. Then, in the same curved section, carve the neighbouring five-sided chip **21** as well as the four-sided chip, as if making a continuation of a larger chip.

Now make a cut at an angle of about 90 degrees that follows the contour of the inner curved line of the curved shape **22**. Then turn the board and make another cut that follows the contour of the outer curved line of the central pattern **23**. Lay the knife close to the surface of the wood and start undercutting the chip along the outer curved line **24**.

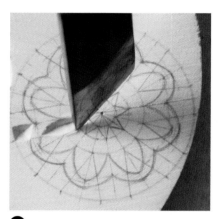

21 Carve the second five-sided chip, then a second four-sided chip.

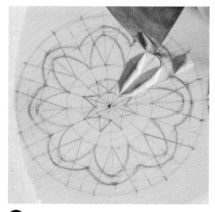

22 Make a cut at an angle of about 90 degrees that follows the contour of the inner curved line.

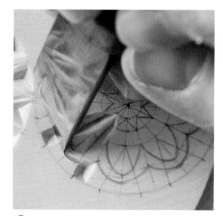

23 Make a cut that follows the contour of the outer curved line of the central pattern.

24 Lay the knife close to the wood surface and start undercutting the chip along the outer curved line.

Since the chip expands from the midpoint, it may not be possible to undercut the chip in one go. Cut the surface with the tip of the knife about 1mm along the perimeter of the outer circle, starting from the middle of the chip **25**, then, in a second stage, finish undercutting the chip **26**.

Turn the board and carve the chip at the inner line. Do this also in two stages: lay the knife close to the surface of the wood and make a straight cut with the tip of the knife **27**, then finish undercutting the chip in the second stage **28**.

The main details in the first section of the pattern are now carved **29**.

25 Lead the tip of the knife along the main circle.

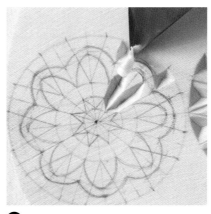

26 Finish undercutting the chip.

27 Make a straight cut with the tip of the knife.

28 Finish undercutting the surface.

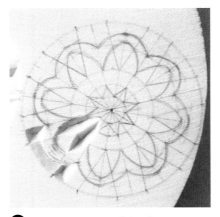

29 The main chips of the first section have been carved.

30 Draw a line from the bottom left corner of the chip to the central dot of the chip that is on the main circle.

31 Make a cut at an angle of about 90 degrees.

Now draw a line by hand from the bottom left corner of the outer chip to the central dot of the chip that is on the main circle **30**. Make a cut at an angle of about 90 degrees **31**, and carve this chip as for carving the base of a straight-wall chip **32**. This step is now carved **33**.

To finish the section, make a cut about 1mm in the middle of the outside chips **34**.

32 Lay the knife close to the wood surface and undercut the chip.

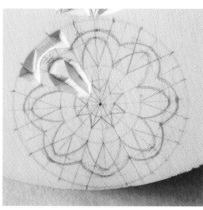

33 This step in the carving is now complete.

34 Make a cut of about 1mm in the middle of the right side of the chip.

Then make two undercuts at an angle of about 60 degrees **35**, **36**. This first section is now almost completely carved **37**.

Repeat all the steps in carving the remaining sections of the pattern.

Finally, start carving the last step in the pattern. Make a straight cut on the right side of a curved section **38**, then lay the knife close to the surface of the wood and make an undercut **39**. Continue between each curved section.

The carving is now complete **40**.

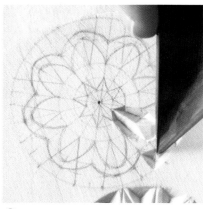

35 Start undercutting the facets of the chip.

36 Make the second undercut.

37 The first section of the pattern has been carved.

38 Make a cut on the right side of the curved section.

39 Lay the knife close to the wood and make an undercut.

40 The pattern is now complete.

Pattern 4

GEMSTONE

The base of this pattern is triangles that are separated from each other by a thin uncut space, and these are then transformed into a complex carving.

TOOLS AND MATERIALS

- Basswood board (at least 100mm square, 1.5mm thick)

- 5mm mechanical pencil with H or HB (#3 or #2) lead

- Ruler

- Compass

- Skew knife

- Sandpaper or leather strips for sharpening

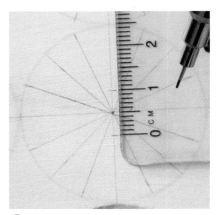

1 Measure a radius of 5mm from the centre of the pattern and draw a circle.

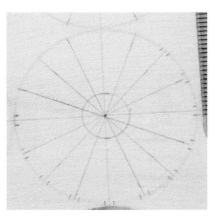

2 Mark dots on the main circle that are 1mm to the right and left of all the straight lines in the pattern.

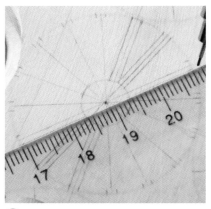

3 Connect the opposite dots together to draw straight lines from circle to circle.

4 Carve all the triangles at an angle of 45 degrees.

5 Mark a dot 1cm from the centre of the pattern on every other line, starting from line 16.

DRAWING PROCESS

First prepare a main circle for the pattern. Using a compass, draw a circle with a radius of 2cm. Then draw two perpendicular lines that intersect at the centre and two diagonal lines that divide the quarters of the circle in half, forming eighths. Now divide the spaces in half again, so you have a circle with 16 identical triangles. Using a pencil and starting from the top of one of the perpendicular lines, mark each of the lines clockwise with numbers: 1, 2, 3. . .16. These marks will help when you are drawing the main pattern.

Measure a radius of 5mm from the centre of the pattern and, using a compass, draw a circle **1**. Next, mark dots on the main circle that are 1mm to the right and left of all the straight lines in the pattern **2**. Connect the opposite dots together, starting at the outer circle and finishing at the inner circle, to make straight lines **3**. The pattern is now ready to begin carving.

CARVING PROCESS

Undercut the sides of the resulting outer triangles at an angle of 45 degrees **4**. Mark a dot 1cm from the centre of the pattern on every other central straight line, starting from line 16 **5**.

Then connect the outer points on top of the odd-numbered lines with the marked dots on the even-numbered lines **6**.

Start carving the contour line pattern. To avoid chipping in places where the facets are connected to each other, you will need to change the grip of the knife when undercutting the sides. The steps here show how to work in one quarter of the pattern at a time.

Start undercutting at an angle of about 65 degrees along an outer long side next to a central straight line, working in a direction towards yourself **7**. Then change the grip of the knife in your hand and cut the outer short side of the chip, working away from you **8**. Without changing the grip of the knife in your hand, cut the outer long side of the chip adjacent to the previously cut chip **9**, working away from you and at an angle of about 65 degrees.

6 Connect the outer points of the odd-numbered lines with the marked dots on the even-numbered lines.

7 Make an undercut at an angle of about 65 degrees along the outer long side of the first chip, working towards yourself.

8 Undercut at an angle of about 65 degrees along the outer short side of the first chip, working away from you.

9 Undercut the outer long side of the second chip, working away from you, at an angle of about 65 degrees.

10 Undercut the outer short side of the second chip, working towards yourself and at an angle of about 65 degrees.

11 Undercut both the inner long and short sides of the first chip together, working towards yourself and at an angle of about 65 degrees.

12 Undercut the inner short side of the second chip at an angle of about 65 degrees.

13 Undercut the inner long side of the second chip at an angle of about 65 degrees.

Now change the grip of the knife in your hand and cut the short side of the second chip, grabbing the previous cut with the tip of the knife **10**.

Next, start undercutting the inner facets of the chips. Cut both the long and short sides of the first chip together, working towards yourself **11**. Then change the knife grip in your hand and cut the short side of the second chip at an angle of about 65 degrees, working away from yourself **12**.

Change the grip of the knife in your hand one more time and finish undercutting the second chip, working at an angle of about 65 degrees **13**.

Next, lay the knife close to the surface of the wood and make a cut on one side of the central straight line in the short space where the long space was divided in half by the contour line carving . Repeat this step on the other side of the space, following the grain direction .

Steps 14 and 15 will result in a sharp edge. To level it, lay your knife close to the surface of the wood and cut the sharp edge with the knife tip .

Draw two lines that form a triangle inside the resulting space . Make two undercuts at an angle of about 65 degrees to carve the triangle .

14 Lay the knife close to the surface of the wood and make a cut on one side of a central line in the reduced space created by the contour line.

15 Make a cut to the other side of the central line in the reduced space, following the grain direction.

16 Cut the sharp edge with the knife tip to level it.

17 Draw two lines to form a triangle inside the newly carved space.

18 Undercut the chip at an angle of about 65 degrees.

19 Make a cut about 2mm long inside the main triangle of the pattern.

20 Make a cut to create a line on top of the short space.

21 Repeat the undercutting steps on the other side of the space

22 Make the first cut starting at the contour line and continue to the centre.

23 Make the second cut of the other side of the same space, from the contour to the centre.

Make a cut about 2mm long inside the main triangle of the pattern, starting at the inner facet of the contour line carving **19**. Then make a cut to carve a line on the top of the short space **20**. Repeat this step on the other side **21**.

To finish carving the pattern in the centre, undercut along the long edges, starting inside the contour line. Make the first cut **22**, and then the second cut on the other side of the same space **23**.

Lay the knife close to the surface of the wood and undercut on one side of the central line  and then on the other side of the central line ㉕. Lay the knife close to the wood surface to remove the sharp edge of the carving ㉖. Repeat the steps to finish the pattern.

The carving is now complete ㉗.

㉔ Lay the knife close to the surface of the wood and undercut on one side of the central line.

㉕ Undercut the chip on the other side of the central line.

㉖ Remove the sharp edge of the carving with the tip of the knife.

㉗ The carving is now complete.

Pattern 5

HIDDEN IN LEAVES

This pattern consists of only multi-level chips, such as double-sided straight-wall chips, as well as two triangles that are connected to each other along adjacent sides, where you will need to make several layers of undercut.

TOOLS AND MATERIALS

- Basswood board (at least 100mm square, 1.5mm thick)

- 5mm mechanical pencil with H or HB (#3 or #2) lead

- Ruler

- Compass

- Skew knife

- Sandpaper or leather strips for sharpening

1 Measure and mark a radius of 1.3cm from the centre of the pattern, then draw a circle.

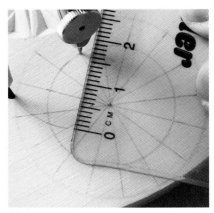

2 Change the radius to 1.65cm, then place the compass on line 5 and, starting at line 1, draw a curved line to the main circle of the pattern.

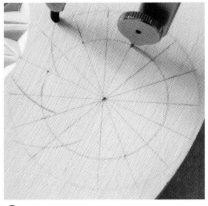

3 Draw curved lines, placing a compass on each odd-numbered line, starting from line 7.

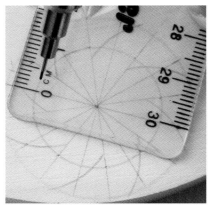

4 Mark dots on the main circle, 3mm to the right of each even-numbered line.

DRAWING PROCESS

First prepare a main circle for the pattern. Using a compass, draw a circle with a radius of 2cm. Then draw two perpendicular lines that intersect at the centre and two diagonal lines that divide the quarters of the circle in half, forming eighths. Now divide the spaces in half again, so you have a circle with 16 identical triangles. Using a pencil and starting from the top of one of the perpendicular lines, mark each of the lines clockwise with numbers: 1, 2, 3. . .16. These marks will help when you are drawing the main pattern.

Measure a radius of 1.3cm from the centre of the pattern and mark it on line 5, then, using a compass, draw a circle **1**. Change the radius of the compass to 1.65cm and place the compass on line 5, where the central circle intersects it, then draw a curve from line 1 to the main outside circle **2**. Without changing the radius and placing the compass on every other point where the central circle intersects the straight odd-numbered lines, draw curved lines, starting from line 7 **3**.

Once these curved lines have been drawn, mark dots on the main circle that are 3mm to the right of each even-numbered line **4**.

Next, make leaf shapes by drawing a second set of curved lines to match up with the first set. Measure a radius of 1.65cm and, placing the compass on one of the dots by the even lines, draw a curve that starts on a line where one of the first curved lines begins and finish the curve at the top of the same first curved line ❺.

Working between two main leaf figures in the pattern, near the triangles that go along the perimeter of the circle, divide one side of each right-hand leaf in half ❻. Then draw a curved line that divides these spaces in half ❼.

Next, measure a radius of 2cm ❽ and then place a compass on the top of line 5 and draw a curved line inside the first figure. Without changing the radius, place the compass at the top of each of the remaining odd-numbered lines, starting from line 7, and draw a curved line inside each shape ❾. The pattern is now ready for carving.

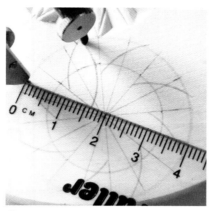

❺ Measure a radius of 1.65cm and, placing a compass on the dots next to the even lines, draw curved lines that join with the first curved lines.

❻ Near the perimeter of the main circle, working between two 'leaves', divide one side of the right-hand leaf in half.

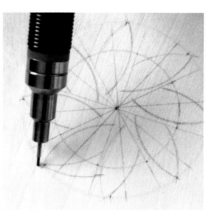

❼ Draw a curved line that divides the triangle space between the 'leaves' in half.

❽ Measure a radius of 2cm.

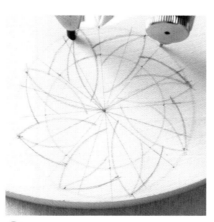

❾ Place a compass on the top of line 5 and draw a curved line inside the first figure.

10 Undercut the outer side of the first triangle at an angle of about 90 degrees.

11 Lay the knife close to the wood surface and undercut the sides of the triangle.

CARVING PROCESS

Begin to carve the pattern with the pairs of triangles that go along the perimeter of the pattern. Undercut the outer side of the first triangle at an angle of about 90 degrees **10**. As these are multi-level triangles, there is no need to undercut the facets too deep, so lay your knife close to the surface of the wood and carve the short and then the long sides **11**. Now undercut the sides of the second triangle that connects to the first one **12**.

Draw the first lines for multi-level carving inside the triangles parallel to their bases **13**. Make cuts on these lines at an angle of about 90 degrees **14**,

12 The first two triangles that are connected to each other have been carved.

13 Draw the lines inside the triangles parallel to their bases.

14 Make cuts on these lines at an angle of about 90 degrees.

Make the first two cuts where the facets of the triangles connect to each other **15**, **16**. Now lay the knife close to the surface of the wood and undercut the sides of the triangles **17**. Repeat these steps two more times to make a multi-level triangle **18**. Continue making multi-level triangles around the pattern.

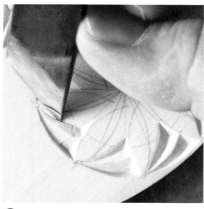

15 Make the first cut where the facets of the triangle connect to each other.

16 Make the second cut, which goes along the perimeter of the circle.

17 Lay the knife close to the wood surface and undercut the side of the triangle.

18 The first multi-level triangle has been carved (shown here at the top).

19 Make a cut along the curved line inside the 'leaf' figures of the pattern at an angle of about 90 degrees.

20 Lay the knife close to the wood surface and undercut the chip.

Start carving the main figures in the pattern. Make a cut along the curved line inside the 'leaf' figures at an angle of about 90 degrees **19**. Then lay the knife close to the surface of the wood and undercut the chip **20**.

Draw three triangles inside the carved space by hand **21**. Cut the sides of the straight-wall chips and carve them **22**. Continue to carve all the main figures in the pattern.

Make cuts between the main 'leaf' figures of the pattern along the straight lines in the centre of the pattern **23**. Then make undercuts at an angle of about 45 degrees **24**.

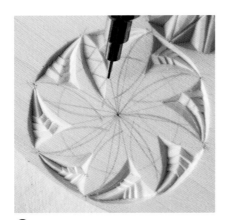

21 Draw three triangles inside the carved chip.

22 Carve the straight-wall chips.

23 Make cuts between the main 'leaf' figures of the pattern.

24 Make undercuts at an angle of about 45 degrees.

The main pattern has been carved **25**.

For the final part of the carving, measure a radius of 1cm and, using a compass, draw lines on the curved spaces of the main figures **26**. Make a cut on a line perpendicular to the wood surface, and then make two undercuts at an angle of about 65 degrees **27**.

The carving is now complete **28**.

25 The main pattern has been carved.

26 Measure a radius of 1cm and, using a compass, draw lines on the curved spaces.

27 Make two undercuts at an angle of about 65 degrees.

28 The carving is now complete.

Pattern 6

NEW MOON

This pattern consists of multi-level chips and contour line carving. It also includes chips where you need to change the angle of the knife when undercutting the facets that go along a line that divides the pattern in half.

TOOLS AND MATERIALS

- Basswood board (at least 100mm square, 1.5mm thick)

- 5mm mechanical pencil with H or HB (#3 or #2) lead

- Ruler

- Compass

- Skew knife

- Sandpaper or leather strips for sharpening

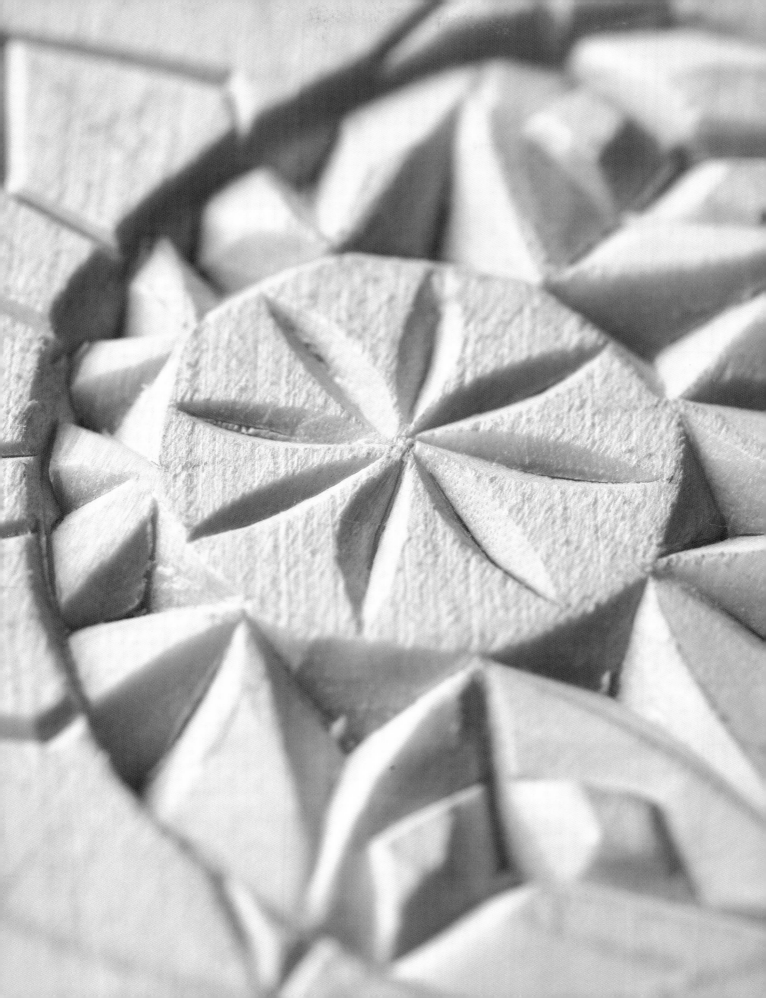

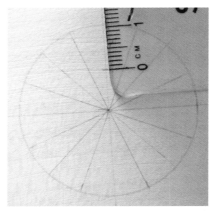

1 Mark a dot on line 5 that is 1.05cm down from the main circle.

2 Draw a curved line using a compass.

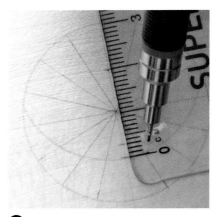

3 Mark a dot on line 13 that is 3mm from the curved line.

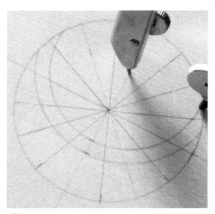

4 Draw a curved line using a compass.

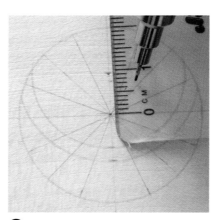

5 Mark a dot on line 5 that is 7.5mm from the centre.

6 Draw a circle using a compass.

DRAWING PROCESS

First prepare a main circle for the pattern. Using a compass, draw a circle with a radius of 2cm. Then draw two perpendicular lines that intersect at the centre and two diagonal lines that divide the quarters of the circle in half, forming eighths. Now divide the spaces in half again, so you have a circle with 16 identical triangles. Using a pencil and starting from the top of one of the perpendicular lines, mark each of the lines clockwise with numbers: 1, 2, 3. . .16. These marks will help when you are drawing the main pattern.

Mark a dot on line 5 that is 1.05cm from the main circle **1**. Then measure a radius of 2cm and, placing the compass on the prepared dot, draw a curved line **2**. Now mark a dot on line 13 that is 3mm from the curved line **3**. Placing the compass on the first prepared dot, draw a curved line that goes through the new dot **4**. Next, mark a dot on line 5 that is 7.5mm from the centre **5** and, using a compass, draw a circle **6**.

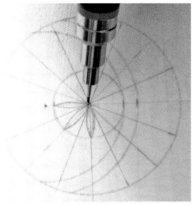

7 Draw ovals with sharp tips inside the central circle.

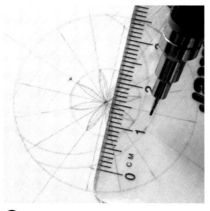

8 Measure a radius of 1.5cm from the centre of the pattern.

9 Mark short lines that intersect every other straight line.

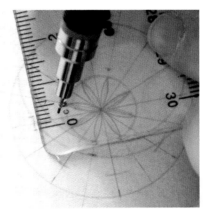

10 Mark a dot on the short lines 1.5mm to the right and left of the long straight lines.

11 Connect the dots to the tops of the straight lines, where they meet the outside circle.

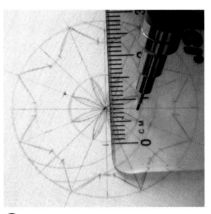

12 Mark a dot 8mm from the centre of the pattern on every other additional line.

In the resulting central circle, starting from line 1, draw two curved lines by hand to the right and left of every other straight line, forming an oval with sharp tips **7**.

Next, measure a radius of 1.5cm from the centre of the pattern **8** and, using a compass, mark short lines that intersect every other long straight line, starting from line 16 **9**. Mark a dot on the resulting short lines that is 1.5mm to the right and left of the long straight lines **10**. Connect the dots to the tops of the long lines, starting from line 1 **11**.

Next, mark a dot 8mm from the centre of the pattern on every other long straight line, starting from line 16 **12**.

13 Connect the dots on the short lines with the new dot that is on the same long straight line.

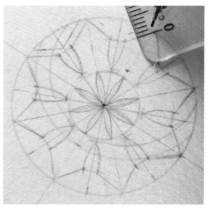

14 Mark a dot 1.5mm from the sides of the main figure of the pattern, then draw lines parallel to the sides.

Connect the resulting dot with the previous prepared dots, drawing a curved line **13**.

Mark a dot 1.5mm from the sides of the main figures of the pattern and draw parallel lines **14**. Next, draw two curved lines inside the main figures of the pattern that form a triangle with a line of the central circle **15**.

The pattern is now ready for carving **16**.

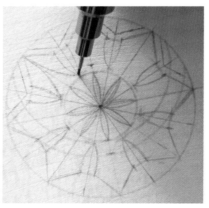

15 Draw two curved lines inside the main figure of the pattern, from the centre at top to the bottom corners.

16 The pattern has been drawn.

CARVING PROCESS

Begin to carve the pattern from the long straight-wall chip that curves through the entire pattern, dividing it into two parts. Undercut the short sides of the straight-wall chip at an angle of about 90 degrees **17**. Then cut the outer line, also at an angle of about 90 degrees, following the grain direction **18**.

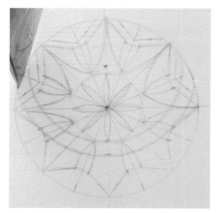

17 Cut the short sides of the straight-wall chip.

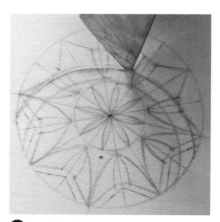

18 Cut the long outer curved side of the straight-wall chip.

Lay the knife close to the surface of the wood and undercut the straight-wall chip, leading the knife along the inner line **19**.

Redraw the lines of the pattern that were removed when carving the straight-wall chip **20**.

Make a stop cut inside the first chip that is partially inside the straight-wall chip **21**. Undercut the short base side at an angle of about 90 degrees **22**. Then carve the sides at an angle of 60–65 degrees **23**. Carve the remaining of these same chips inside the straight-wall chip.

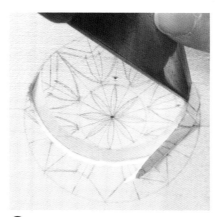

19 Undercut the straight-wall chip following the grain direction.

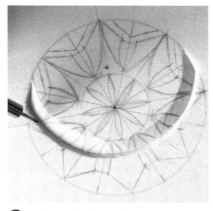

20 Redraw the lines of the pattern that were removed when carving the straight-wall chip.

21 Make a stop cut inside the chip that is partially inside the straight-wall chip.

22 Cut the base of the chip.

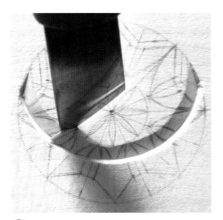

23 Carve the sides of the chip at an angle of 60–65 degrees.

24 Make a stop cut inside the eight-sided chip.

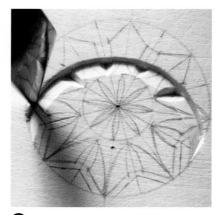

25 Cut the short sides of the chip.

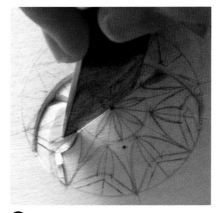

26 Finish carving the eight-sided chip.

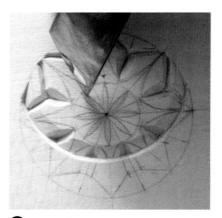

27 Carve the two-sided chips at an angle of about 65 degrees.

28 Carve the three-sided chips at an angle of about 45 degrees.

29 Draw two short lines by hand that form a rhombus with a point in the triangles as shown.

Next, start undercutting the eight-sided chips that go around the main figures of the patterns (these look like a three-arm windmill). First make a stop cut inside the chip **24**.

Next, cut the thin parts of the eight-sided chip at an angle of about 65 degrees. Where the short sides go along the curved side of the straight-wall chip, undercut the sides at an angle of about 90 degrees **25**. Finish carving the chip at its widest place, undercutting the facets at an angle of about 65 degrees **26**.

Carve the two-sided chips inside the central circle at an angle of about 65 degrees **27**.

Next, carve the three-sided chips inside the main figures at an angle of about 45 degrees **28**. Where the three-sided chips go inside the straight-wall chip and 'transform' into four-sided chips, undercut the short sides at an angle of about 90 degrees.

Draw two short lines by hand that are parallel to the sides of a triangle to form a rhombus **29**. Cut the resulting lines at an angle of about 90 degrees **30**.

30 Cut the lines at an angle of about 90 degrees.

31 Lay the knife close to the surface of the wood and make the first cut.

32 Make the second cut following the grain direction.

33 Undercut the inner facets at an angle of about 65 degrees.

34 Finish carving the contour line carving.

35 The carving is now complete.

Then lay the knife close to the surface of the wood and make two cuts following the grain direction **31**, **32**.

Carve the contour lines, starting from the inner facets at an angle of about 65 degrees **33**. Then undercut the outer facets **34**.

The carving is now complete **35**.

Pattern 7

A FLOWER IN SNOW

This pattern creates a series of patterns where it is necessary to cut the space between two circles in such a way as to get a smooth surface.

TOOLS AND MATERIALS

- Basswood board (at least 100mm square, 1.5mm thick)

- 5mm mechanical pencil with H or HB (#3 or #2) lead

- Ruler

- Compass

- Skew knife

- Sandpaper or leather strips for sharpening

1 Mark three dots at 1.6cm, 9mm and 8mm from the centre of the pattern on any straight line.

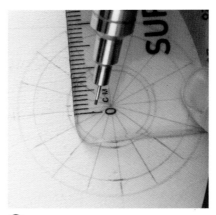

2 Mark a dot 1mm to the right and left of each straight line on the second central circle.

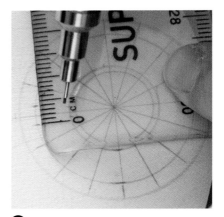

3 Mark a dot 2mm to the right and left of each straight line on the third circle inside the pattern.

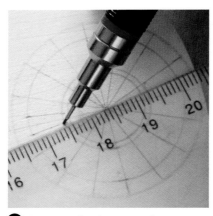

4 Connect the dots together between the second and third circles.

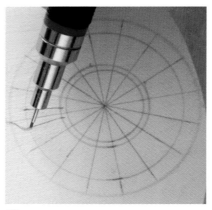

5 Draw an undulating curved line connecting the dots on the third circle with the top of the straight line next to them.

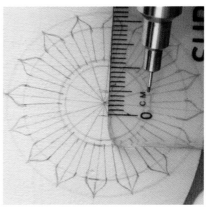

6 Measure a radius of 2.5mm from the centre of the pattern and draw a circle.

DRAWING PROCESS

First prepare a main circle for the pattern. Using a compass, draw a circle with a radius of 2cm. Then draw two perpendicular lines that intersect at the centre and two diagonal lines that divide the quarters of the circle in half, forming eighths. Now divide the spaces in half again, so you have a circle with 16 identical triangles. Using a pencil and starting from the top of one of the perpendicular lines,

mark each of the lines clockwise with numbers: 1, 2, 3. . .16. These marks will help when you are drawing the main pattern.

Measure three radius from the centre of the pattern on any straight line at 1.6cm, 9mm and 8mm **1**. Then, using a compass, draw three circles.

Mark a dot 1mm to the right and left of each straight line on second central circle **2**. Next,

mark a dot 2mm to the right and left of each straight line on the third circle of the pattern **3**. Connect the resulting dots together **4**. Then draw slightly undulating curved lines that connect the dots on the third circle with the top of the straight lines **5**.

Measure a radius of 2.5mm from the centre of the pattern and draw a circle **6**.

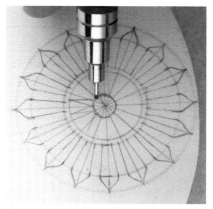

7 Draw triangles in each of the 16 spaces between the first and second central circles.

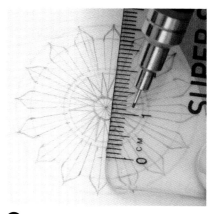

8 Mark a dot on line 14 that is 1.1cm from the centre of the pattern.

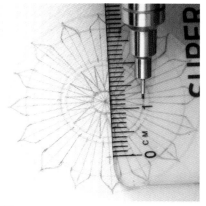

9 Mark a dot on line 15 that is 1.2cm from the centre of the pattern.

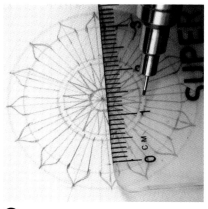

10 Mark a dot on line 16 that is 1.4cm from the centre of the pattern.

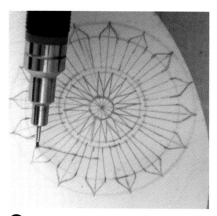

11 Connect the dots by drawing a curved line.

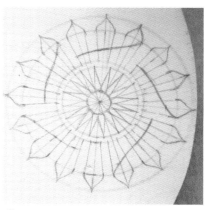

12 Draw more curved lines to make further petals.

Draw triangles in each of the 16 spaces between the first and second central circles **7**.

Mark three dots: make the first dot 1.1cm from the centre of the pattern on line 14 **8**; the second, 1.2cm from the centre of the pattern on line 15 **9**; the third, 1.4cm from the centre of the pattern on line 16 **10**. Draw a curved line connecting the resulting dots and lead it to the point where the fourth circle intersects the top of the petal on line 16 **11**. Repeat these steps to make further petals **12**.

13 Draw two curved lines inside the petal centred on line 13.

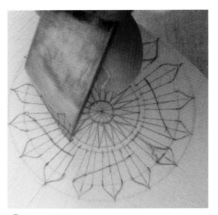

14 Undercut the base of a six-sided chip at an angle of about 60 degrees.

15 Undercut the long side of a six-sided chip at an angle of about 60 degrees.

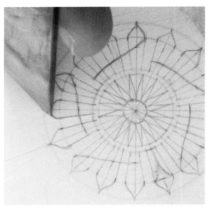

16 Undercut the curved facet at an angle of about 60 degrees.

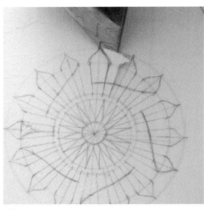

17 Undercut the top of the chip at an angle of about 45 degrees.

Draw two curved lines inside the petal on line 13, starting with the points where the fourth circle intersects the top of the petal, and connect them together at the base of the petal **13**.

CARVING PROCESS

Begin to carve the pattern from the spaces between the petals. Undercut the short side of a six-sided chip at an angle of about 60 degrees **14**, then cut a long side of the chip **15** and finish the side at the curved facet **16**. Repeat this along the other side of the chip and then undercut the top of the chip at an angle of about 45 degrees **17**.

Undercutting the space between two circles
Make a cut along the entire perimeter of the outer circle at an angle of about 90 degrees. Then mentally divide the space between the two circles into quarters. All the following undercuts will be straight cuts, with the tip of the knife going around the perimeter of the circle.

Lay the knife close to the surface of the wood and carve the top left quarter away from you, leading the knife along the line of the inner circle. Then carve the opposite quarter, also away from you. Undercut the remaining quarters towards yourself. Then level the space with additional straight cuts to get a smooth surface.

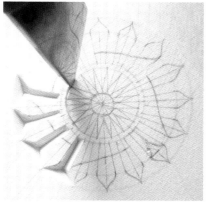

18 Make a cut along the perimeter of the second circle.

19 Make a first undercut working away from yourself.

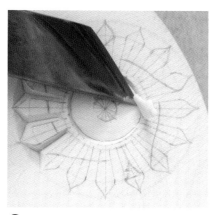

20 Finish undercutting the surface towards yourself.

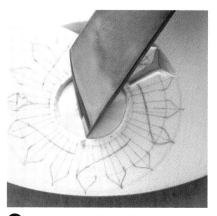

21 Level the surface with straight cuts.

22 Redraw triangles inside the carved space.

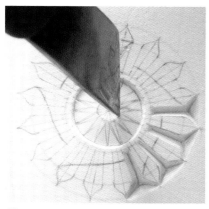

23 Undercut the base of the triangles at an angle of 60–65 degrees.

Make a cut along the entire perimeter of the second central circle at an angle of about 90 degrees **18**. Start the first cut by working away from yourself and finish undercutting the last quarter towards yourself **19**, **20**. Level the space by making additional straight cuts to get a smooth surface **21**.

Redraw the triangles that were removed while carving inside the central cricle **22**.

In the central section, start carving the triangles from the base at an angle of 60–65 degrees **23**.

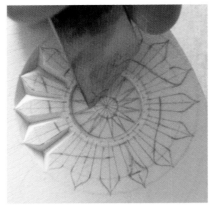

24 Carve the facets of the triangles at an angle of 60–65 degrees.

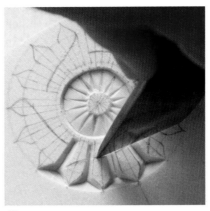

25 Make a cut on the lines that go along the main petals of the pattern.

26 Make an undercut at an angle of about 30 degrees.

27 Carve the petals on either side of the central line with a straight cut.

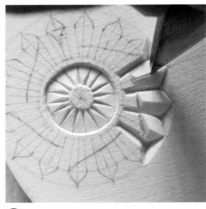

28 Make a cut on the central line of the petals.

Then undercut the sides of the triangles, also at an angle of 60–65 degrees **24**.

Make a cut on the lines that go along the main petals of the pattern **25**. Then undercut it at an angle of about 30 degrees **26**.

Next, place the knife close to the surface of the wood and carve the petals on either side of the central line, making a straight cut **27**.

Make a cut on the central line of the petals. When the knife tip is about 2mm from the top of the petals, stop here **28**.

29 Undercut the base of the cut.

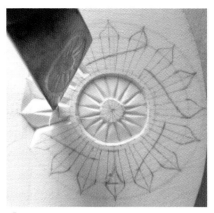

30 Make two undercuts at an angle of about 65 degrees.

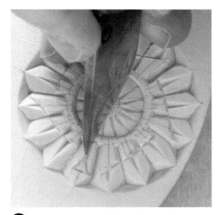

31 On line 13, make cuts on the curved lines inside the petal at an angle of about 90 degrees.

32 Undercut the half rhombus in the same way as for carving the base of a straight-wall chip.

33 The carving is now complete.

Then use the tip to make an undercut at the base of the previous cut **29**.

Now make two undercuts at an angle of about 65 degrees **30**.

To finish the pattern, make cuts on the curved lines inside the petal on line 13, at an angle of about 90 degrees **31**. Finally, undercut the half rhombus in the same way as for carving the base of a straight-wall chip **32**.

The pattern is now complete **33**.

TWO FEATHERS

This pattern consists of both multi-level chips and a central pattern in the form of a spiral, where it is necessary to work only using the tip of the knife.

TOOLS AND MATERIALS

- Basswood board (at least 100mm square, 1.5mm thick)

- 5mm mechanical pencil with H or HB (#3 or #2) lead

- Ruler

- Compass

- Skew knife

- Sandpaper or leather strips for sharpening

1 Mark three dots from the centre of the pattern at 1.7cm, 1.2cm and 8mm, then draw three circles.

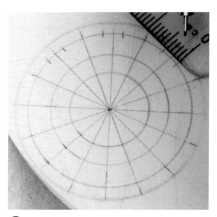

2 Starting on line 1, mark a dot 2mm to the left and right of every odd-numbered straight line.

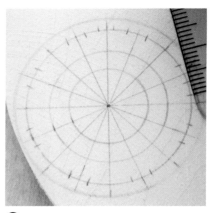

3 Mark another set of dots that are 3mm from the first set of dots.

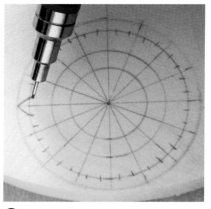

4 Connect the top of line 1 with the nearest dots on the third circle of the pattern.

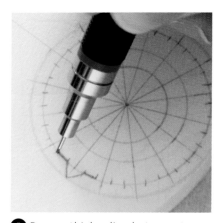

5 Draw a thicker line between two neighbouring dots to define the lines.

DRAWING PROCESS

First prepare a main circle for the pattern. Using a compass, draw a circle with a radius of 2cm. Then draw two perpendicular lines that intersect at the centre and two diagonal lines that divide the quarters of the circle in half, forming eighths. Now divide the spaces in half again, so you have a circle with 16 identical triangles. Using a pencil and starting from the top of one of the perpendicular lines, mark each of the lines clockwise with numbers: 1, 2, 3. . .16. These marks will help when you are drawing the main pattern.

Mark three dots: make the first dot 1.7cm from the centre of the pattern; the second, 1.2cm from the centre of the pattern; and the third, 8mm from the centre of the pattern. Using a compass, draw three circles from these dots **1**.

Next, starting from line 1, mark a dot 2mm to the left and right of every odd-numbered line on the main circle of the pattern **2**. Mark a dot 3mm from these resulting dots **3**.

Now start drawing the main pattern. Connect the top of line 1 with the dots on the third circle of the pattern that are to the right and left of line 1 **4**. To define the lines of the pattern, draw thicker lines from the dots to the right and left of line 1 to the dots that are next to them **5**.

Mark a dot 3mm to the right and left of line 16 on the second circle of the pattern and on every odd-numbered line, starting from line 16 **6**. Connect the ends of the lines on the third circle of the pattern with the resulting dots on the second circle, drawing curved lines **7**. Now connect the tips of the lines that are on the third circle of the pattern to the top of every even-numbered line, starting from line 16 **8**.

Next, draw a curved line from the top of line 15 to the dot where the first circle of the pattern intersects line 14 **9**. Then draw a curved line from the top of line 15 to the dot where the first circle of the pattern crosses line 16. Repeat this with the top of every odd-numbered line, starting from line 1.

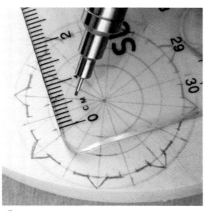

6 Mark dots on the second circle of the pattern that are 3mm to the right and left of line 16.

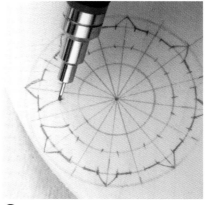

7 Connect the ends of the lines on the third circle with the dots that are on the second circle.

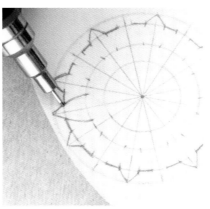

8 Connect the tips of the lines that are on the third circle of the pattern to the top of every other line.

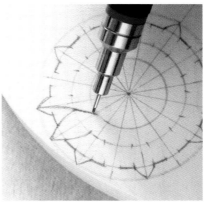

9 Draw a curved line from the top of line 15 to the point where the first circle intersects with line 14.

10 Mark a dot on line 9 that is 7mm from the centre of the pattern.

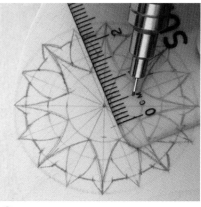

11 Mark a dot on line 8 that is 5mm from the centre of the pattern.

Next, mark four dots: make the first dot 7mm from the centre of the pattern on line 9 **10**.

Mark the second dot 5mm from the centre of the pattern on line 8 **11**; the third, 4mm from the centre of the pattern on line 7 **12**; and the fourth, 3mm from the centre of the pattern on line 6 **13**.

Connect the resulting dots by drawing a curved line, starting from the point where the first circle of the pattern intersects line 10 and ending with the centre of the pattern **14**. Repeat these steps for every odd-numbered line, starting with line 7 **15**.

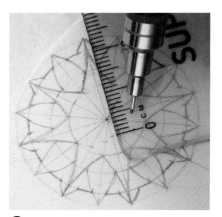

12 Mark a dot on line 7 that is 4mm from the centre of the pattern.

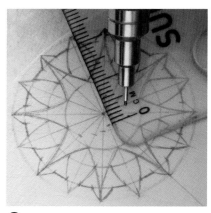

13 Mark a dot on line 6 that is 3mm from the centre of the pattern.

14 Connect the dots to the centre point, starting from the dot where the first circle of the pattern intersects with line 10.

15 Draw the rest of the swirl pattern.

CARVING PROCESS

Begin carving the pattern at the three-sided straight-wall chips that go around the perimeter of the pattern. First, cut the sides of the rhombuses **16**, then cut the central top side **17**. Now lay the knife close to the surface of the wood and carve the straight-wall chip **18**.

Next, start carving the central spiral pattern from the sides that go along the grain. Make a cut in the direction towards yourself at an angle of about 65 degrees **19**, then change the grip of the knife in your hand and cut the side along the most curved point at an angle of about 45 degrees **20**.

16 Cut the sides of a straight-wall chip that connect to the points of the rhombuses.

17 Cut the central top side of a straight-wall chip.

18 Carve a straight-wall chip.

19 Make a cut, working towards yourself, at an angle of about 65 degrees.

20 Cut the side along the most curved point at an angle of about 45 degrees.

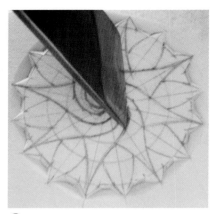

21 Finish cutting along this facet of the chip.

22 Undercut the base of the three-sided chip.

Change the grip of the knife one more time in your hand and finish cutting this side of the chip **21**.

Then undercut the base of the curved triangle, working in the direction away from you at an angle of about 45 degrees **22**. Start carving the last long side of the triangle, working in the direction away from you at an angle of about 45 degrees **23**, leading the knife to the most curved point of the facet **24**.

23 Start undercutting the last long facet of the chip, working away from yourself.

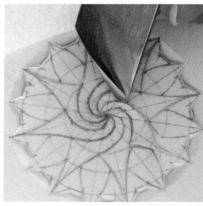

24 Lead the knife towards the most curved point of the facet.

Now change the grip of the knife in your hand and finish carving the thin part of the chip at an angle of about 65 degrees **25**. The first curved triangle has been carved **26**. Continue carving the spiral pattern clockwise **27**.

Next, cut the side of a rhombus at an angle of about 90 degrees **28**. Then lay the knife close to the surface of the wood and undercut a curved triangle, as for carving a base of a straight-wall chip, following the grain direction of the wood **29**.

25 Finish undercutting along this facet, in the thin part of the chip.

26 The first curved triangle of the central pattern has been carved.

27 Continue carving the curved chips clockwise.

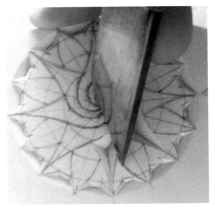

28 Cut the side of a rhombus at an angle of about 90 degrees.

29 Undercut a curved triangle, following the grain direction of the wood.

30 Start cutting the left side of the rhombus.

31 Finish cutting around the left side of the rhombus.

Start cutting the left side of the rhombus at an angle of about 90 degrees **30**, then, without removing the tip of the knife from the wood, finish cutting the left side of the rhombus **31**. Lay the knife close to the surface of the wood and undercut one half of the rhombus **32**.

The last stage in the carving of the pattern is to carve multi-level chips along the perimeter of the main circle. Draw two lines that form two triangles inside the straight-wall chips between lines 1 and line 9 **33**. Then carve the two straight-wall chips.

32 Undercut one half of the rhombus.

33 Draw two lines to form two triangles inside the straight-wall chips between lines 1 and 9.

Cut the straight-wall chips between lines 10 and 16 by placing the knife on the point where the side of the rhombus intersects the short line of the curved triangle and cutting to the base of the chip at the long side of the curved triangle **34**. Carve the straight-wall chip **35**.

Next, mentally divide the side of the previous straight-wall chip in half, and make a cut anticlockwise from it **36**, then undercut the chip **37**. Continue to finish the pattern.

The carving is now complete **38**.

34 Make a cut from the point where the side of the rhombus intersects the short line of the curved triangle to the base of the chip at the long side of the curved triangle.

35 Carve the straight-wall chip.

36 Make a cut anticlockwise from the previous straight-wall chip.

37 Carve the straight-wall chip.

38 The carving is now complete.

LAST SNOWFLAKE

This pattern is based on the sharp edges of the carving, but it also consists of chips with a rounded side that go along the grain, and once again you will need to look for an invisible point to get a smooth surface on a facet.

TOOLS AND MATERIALS

- Basswood board (at least 100mm square, 1.5mm thick)

- 5mm mechanical pencil with H or HB (#3 or #2) lead

- Ruler

- Compass

- Skew knife

- Sandpaper or leather strips for sharpening

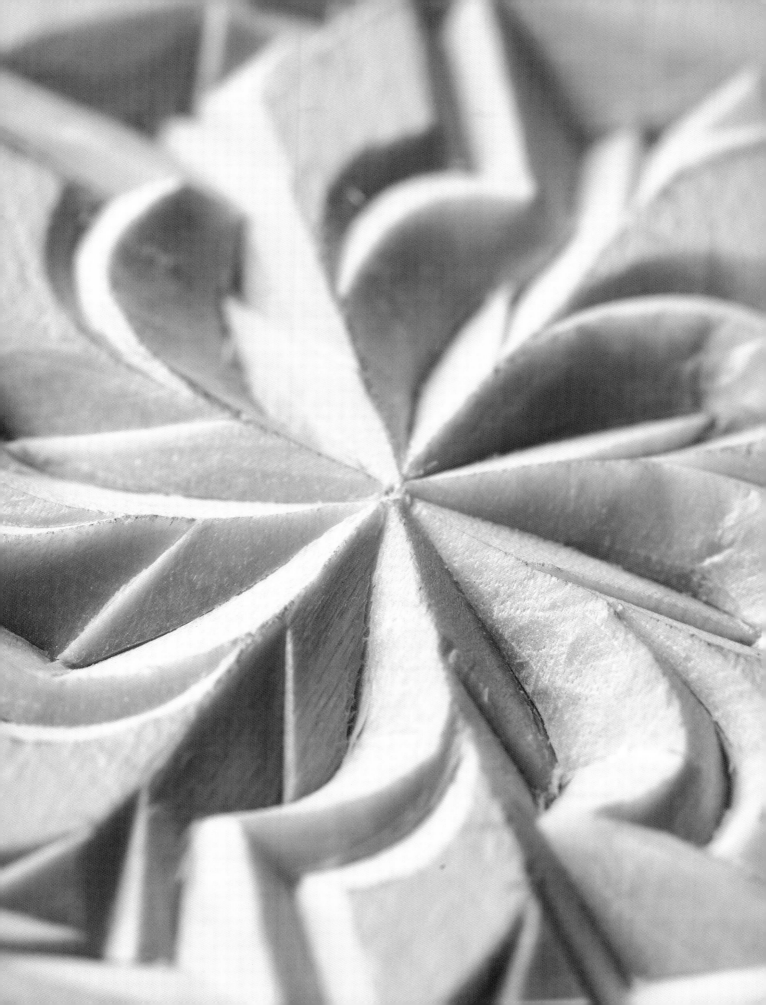

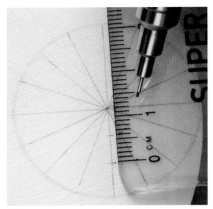

1 Mark two dots from the centre of the pattern and draw two circles.

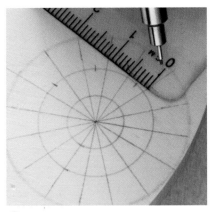

2 Divide every other space between the lines, starting in the space between lines 1 and 2.

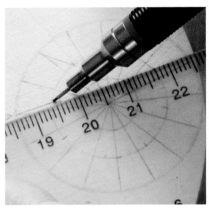

3 Connect the dots with the tops of the lines on the left.

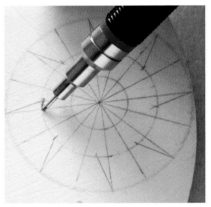

4 Define the short lines on the second circle of the pattern.

DRAWING PROCESS

First prepare a main circle for the pattern. Using a compass, draw a circle with a radius of 2cm. Then draw two perpendicular lines that intersect at the centre and two diagonal lines that divide the quarters of the circle in half, forming eighths. Now divide the spaces in half again, so you have a circle with 16 identical triangles. Using a pencil and starting from the top of one of the perpendicular lines, mark each of the lines clockwise with numbers: 1, 2, 3. . .16. These marks will help when you are drawing the main pattern.

Mark two dots on any straight line: make the first dot 1.2cm from the centre of the pattern; the second, 6mm from the centre **1**. Now draw two circles.

Starting with the space between lines 1 and 2, divide every other space between the lines in half, making marks on the second circle **2**. Connect the resulting dots with the tops of the lines on the left, so if the dot is between line 1 and line 2, connect the dot to line 1 **3**. Now, to define the lines, draw a thicker line from the dots on the second circle of the pattern to the point the same circle intersects the straight lines **4**.

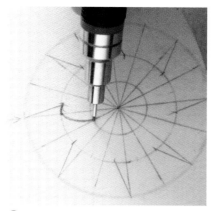

5 Draw a curved line by hand from the point where the second circle intersects line 1 to the point where the first circle intersects line 16.

6 Mark a dot 2mm to the left of the straight line and another 2mm to the left of the curved line.

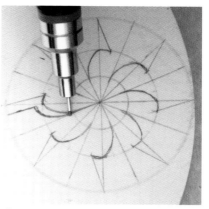

7 Draw the straight line and connect the curved line to it and where the first circle of the pattern intersects line 16.

8 Mark a dot 1.4cm from the centre of the pattern on every even-numbered line, starting at line 16.

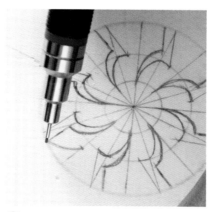

9 Connect the dot to the top of the line that is next to it on the right.

Then draw a curved line by hand from the dot where the second circle intersects line 1 to the point where the first circle intersects line 16 **5**. Repeat this with every odd-numbered line, starting from line 15. Mark a dot 2mm to the left of the straight line and another 2mm to the left of the curved line and draw parallel lines **6**, connecting the end of the curved line to the point where the first circle intersects line 16 **7**.

Starting from line 16, mark a dot 1.4cm from the centre of the pattern on every even-numbered line **8**. Connect the resulting dot to the top of the line that is next to it on the right **9**. The pattern is ready to start carving.

10 Undercut the long side at an angle of about 60 degrees.

11 Undercut the base of the chip at an angle of about 45 degrees.

12 Place the knife close at the long side and undercut the short facet of the chip.

13 Start undercutting the curved facet of the chip from the centre of the pattern.

14 Carve the most curved part of the facet, leading the knife and connecting the cut to the previous one already made.

15 Make a cut at the base of the large four-sided chip.

CARVING PROCESS

Begin to carve the pattern in a large four-sided chip – it has a long straight side and is curved on the other side, in the half near the centre of the pattern. Undercut the long side at an angle of about 60 degrees **10**.

Push the knife deep into the wood at the widest place of the chip. Then cut the base of the chip at an angle of about 45 degrees **11**.

Place the knife close at the long side and undercut the short facet of the chip **12**. Then start undercutting the curved facet of the chip from the centre of the pattern **13**. If the chip goes along the grain, then change the grip of the knife in your hand and start carefully carving the most curved part of the facet, leading the knife and connecting the cut to the previous one **14** (see the technique of undercutting a curved side that goes along the grain, which I wrote for the second pattern).

Place the knife about 2mm from the short line and make a cut at the base of the chip **15**.

16 Make a cut parallel to the short side of the large four-sided chip.

17 Carve the straight-wall chip.

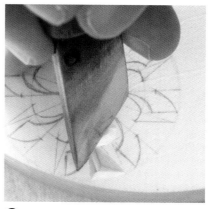

18 Cut the sides of the chip at an angle of about 90 degrees.

19 Carve the straight-wall chip.

20 Make a cut in the middle of the common base of the straight-wall chips with the tip of a knife.

21 Now make two cuts on one and the other side of the cut.

Then change the knife grip in your hand and make a cut parallel to the short side of the four-sided chip, starting from the beginning of the previous cut **16**.

Carve the resulting straight-wall chip **17**.

Next, carve another straight-wall chip, this time the chip in the main shape of the pattern, where its base is connected to the base of the previously cut straight-wall chip. Cut the sides of the chip at an angle of about 90 degrees **18**. Then carve the straight-wall chip **19**.

Using the tip of the knife, make a cut in the middle of the common base of the straight-wall chips **20**. Now make two cuts, one on either side of the cut **21**.

22 Make a stop cut inside the thin five-sided chip.

23 Undercut the short base of the thin five-sided chip.

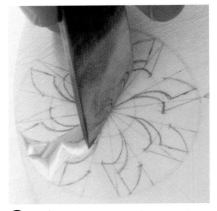

24 Start undercutting the curved facet at the most curved point, working towards yourself.

25 Finish undercutting the curved facet, working away from yourself.

26 Undercut the side that is next to the curved facet.

27 Start cutting the straight side, starting from the curved side.

Next, make a stop cut inside the thin five-sided chip, where two faces meet each other, to avoid chipping in this place when undercutting the sides **22**.

Cut the short side, or base, of the chip at an angle of about 60 degrees **23**.

Next, start undercutting the curved facet at the most curved point, leading the knife towards the centre of the pattern **24**.

Change the knife grip in your hand and finish undercutting the curved facet by carefully leading the tip of the knife to the stop cut **25**. Then undercut the side that is next to the curved facet **26**.

Turn the board and cut the straight side, starting from the curved side **27**.

28 Finish carving the thin five-sided chip, undercutting the curved facet.

29 About 3mm from the top of the curved line, place the knife on the long facet and make a cut.

30 Make a cut at the top of the curved line.

31 Carve the straight-wall chip.

32 The first section of the pattern has been carved.

33 The carving is now complete.

Finish carving the thin five-sided chip by undercutting the curved facet, starting from the straight side of the chip **28**.

Next, carve a straight-wall chip inside the already carved, large four-sided chip. To do this, place the knife about 3mm from the top of the curved line at an angle of about 90 degrees on the long facet and make a cut that ends at the line of the first circle **29**.

Then make a cut at the top of the curved line **30** and carve the straight-wall chip **31**. The first section of the pattern has been carved **32**. Repeat the steps to carve the remaining sections.

The carving is now complete **33**.

Pattern 10

COMPASS OF LOVE

The complexity of carving this pattern lies in the sequence of steps you need to make as you move from one chip to another.

TOOLS AND MATERIALS

- Basswood board (at least 100mm square, 1.5mm thick)

- 5mm mechanical pencil with H or HB (#3 or #2) lead

- Ruler

- Compass

- Skew knife

- Sandpaper or leather strips for sharpening

1 Mark a dot 3mm from the main circle on the four perpendicular lines.

2 Mark a dot 1.3cm from the centre on the four perpendicular lines.

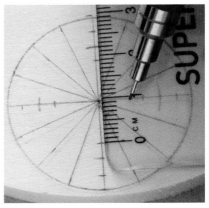

3 Mark a dot 9.5mm from the centre on the four perpendicular lines.

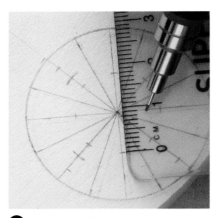

4 Mark a dot 9mm from the centre on the 4 diagonal lines.

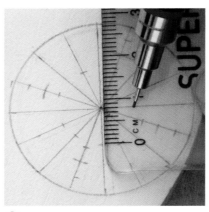

5 Mark a dot 8mm from the centre on the lines on the right and left sides of the perpendicular lines.

DRAWING PROCESS

First prepare a main circle for the pattern. Using a compass, draw a circle with a radius of 2cm. Then draw two perpendicular lines that intersect at the centre and two diagonal lines that divide the quarters of the circle in half, forming eighths. Now divide the spaces in half again, so you have a circle with 16 identical triangles. Using a pencil and starting from the top of one of the perpendicular lines, mark each of the lines clockwise with numbers: 1, 2, 3. . .16. These marks will help when you are drawing the main pattern.

Mark a dot 3mm from the main circle of the pattern on four perpendicular lines: 1, 5, 9 and 13 **1**. Now mark a dot 1.3cm from the centre of the pattern on the same four perpendicular lines **2**. Then mark a dot 9.5mm from the centre of the pattern also on the same perpendicular lines **3**.

Next, mark a dot 9mm from the centre on four diagonal lines: 3, 7, 11 and 15 **4**.

Mark a dot 8mm from the centre on line 16, then on lines 2, 4, 6, 8, 10, 12 and 14 (all the even-numbered lines) **5**.

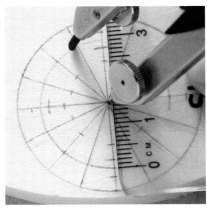

6 Measure a radius of 1.5cm from the centre of the pattern and draw a circle.

7 Mark two dots on the second circle that are 2mm to the right and left of the perpendicular lines.

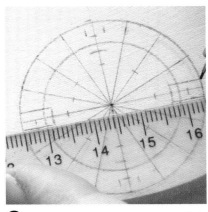

8 Draw short lines that are parallel to the perpendicular lines.

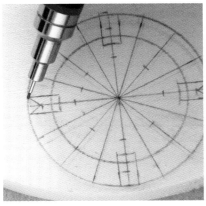

9 Connect the dot between the short lines, on the perpendicular line, with the points on the main circle.

10 Connect the dot on the perpendicular line closest to the centre to the ends of the short parallel lines.

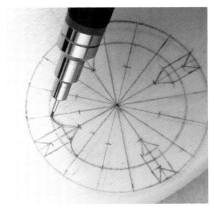

11 Draw curved lines to the points where the first circle intersects lines 16 and 2.

Measure a radius of 1.5cm from the centre of the pattern and draw a circle **6**.

Mark a dot 2mm to the right and left of the perpendicular lines of the pattern **7** and draw parallel lines to the second dots that are 1.3cm from the centre of the pattern **8**, then draw a short line between the 1.3cm dots.

Now connect the dot on the perpendicular line, 3mm from the outside circle, with the dots on the main circle and to the right and left of the perpendicular line **9**. Connect the dot 9.5mm from the centre of the pattern, on the perpendicular line, to the ends of the parallel lines **10**.

Next, draw curved lines from the ends of the parallel lines to the points where the first circle of the main pattern intersects lines 16 and 2 **11**.

Repeat these steps with the remaining perpendicular lines of the pattern.

12 Connect the points where the first circle intersects lines 16 and 2 with the dots on the same lines.

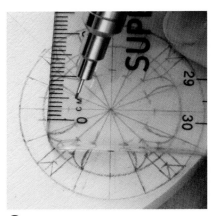

13 Mark a dot 2.5mm to the right and left of the diagonal lines on the first circle.

14 Connect the two dots to the one on the diagonal line between them.

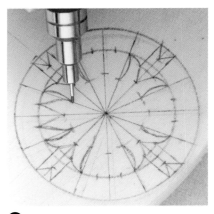

15 Connect the dots to the right and left of the diagonal line to the dots that are on lines 2 and 4.

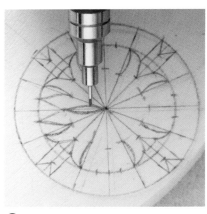

16 Draw two curved lines to form an oval with sharp points.

17 The pattern is now ready for carving.

Next, connect the points where the first circle of the pattern intersects line 16 and line 2 with the dots on the same lines **12**.

Mark two dots on the first circle 2.5mm to the right and left of the diagonal lines **13**. Connect the resulting dots with the dot on the diagonal line between them **14**. Now connect the dots that are to the right and left of the diagonal line of with the dots on line 2 and line 4 **15**. Draw two curved lines from the dot on the same diagonal line to the centre of the pattern, forming an oval with sharp points **16**.

Repeat all the steps in the remaining sections of the pattern **17**. The pattern is now ready for carving.

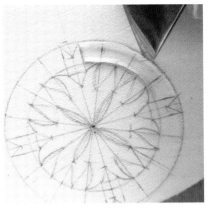

18 Undercut all sides of a curved four-sided chip at an angle of about 60 degrees.

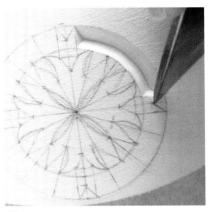

19 Cut the side of a straight-wall chip.

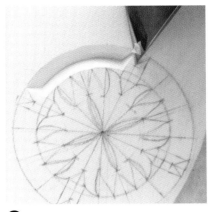

20 Carve the straight-wall chip.

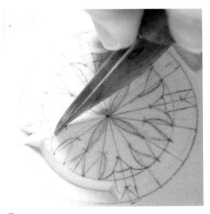

21 Make a straight cut that goes from the short side of the curved four-sided chip to the point where two main petals of the pattern connect to each other.

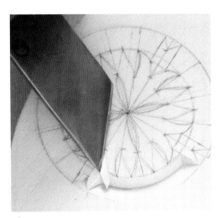

22 Make a cut on one side of the previous cut.

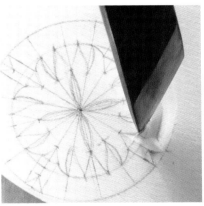

23 Make a rounded cut that follows the shape of the petal.

CARVING PROCESS

Begin to carve the pattern around the perimeter of the main circle, starting with curved four-sided chips. Undercut all sides at an angle of about 60 degrees **18**.

Cut the sides of a straight-wall chip that is on a perpendicular line in the pattern **19**, then carve the straight-wall chip **20**.

Make a straight cut that goes from the short side of the curved four-sided chip to the point where two main petals of the pattern connect to each other **21**.

Lay the knife close to the surface of the wood and make a cut on one side of the previous cut, working either away from yourself or towards yourself, depending on which direction the knife goes smoothly through the grain **22**.

Make a rounded cut that follows the shape of the petal **23**.

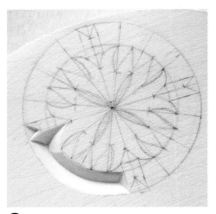

24 The first stage of the carving is complete.

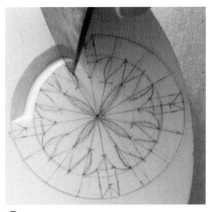

25 Adjoining the large curved chip, cut the sides of the three straight-wall chips.

26 Carve the straight-wall chips.

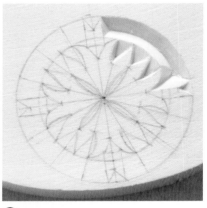

27 The first three straight-wall chips have been carved.

28 Draw two curved lines inside the main petals of the pattern.

29 Carve a two-sided chip at an angle of about 65 degrees.

The first stage with the curved four-sided chip is complete **24**.

Next, cut the sides of the three straight-wall chips that connect with their bases to the inner side of a curved four-sided chip **25**. Carve the straight-wall chips **26**. The first three straight-wall chips have been carved **27**.

Now draw curved lines inside the main petals about 1mm from the sides, following the lines of the petals **28**. Carve the resulting two-sided chips at an angle of about 65 degrees **29**.

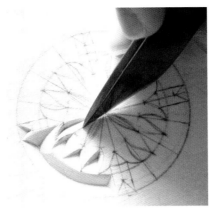

30 Make the first cuts perpendicular to the surface of the wood on one side of a rhombus.

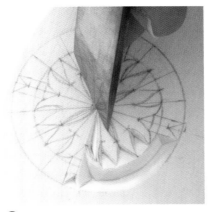

31 Make a cut perpendicular to the surface of the wood on the other side of a rhombus.

32 Make a cut by eye on one side of the rhombus.

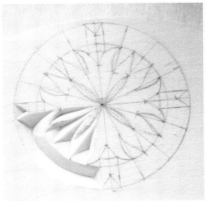

33 The first two chips with sharp edges have been carved.

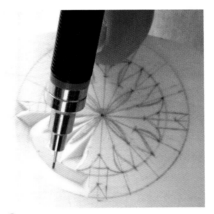

34 Mark two dots on the inner long facet of a curved four-sided chip.

35 Draw a curved line from the dot to the opposite chip.

Make cuts perpendicular to the surface of the wood at the rhombuses near the diagonal lines **30**, **31**. Draw central lines inside the rhombuses before undercutting the sides, or make two cuts by eye on one side of the rhombus and then on the other **32**, **33**.

The next stage adds another layer to the perimeter of the pattern. First, mentally draw a line from the tips of the chips with sharp edges, then mark two dots where the long facets of the curved four-sided chip meet each other **34**.

Draw a curved line from one dot to the opposite chip, making a line that goes through the base of the chip to the side of the chip with sharp edges **35**.

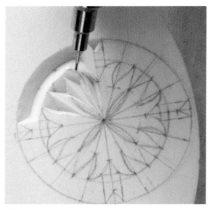

36 Draw a curved line from the same dot to the top of the petal.

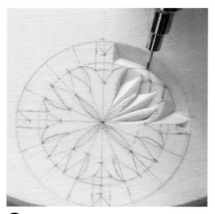

37 Draw two lines from the second dot inside the curved four-sided chip.

38 Undercut the inner facet that goes along the grain.

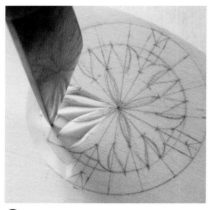

39 Start undercutting the outer facet that goes against the grain.

40 Finish undercutting the outer facet that go against the grain.

Now draw a curved line from the same dot to the top of the petal **36**. Repeat these steps with the other dot **37**.

Start undercutting the facets of the contour line carving from the side that goes along the grain at an angle of about 65 degrees **38**, then undercut the facet that connects to the previous one **39**.

Now change the grip of the knife and finish undercutting the second facet **40**.

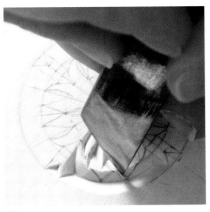

41 Undercut the outer facet of the chip that goes against the grain.

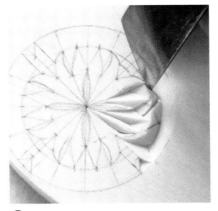

42 Undercut the outer facet of the chip that goes along the grain.

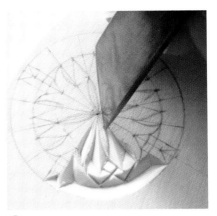

43 Cut one side of an oval.

44 Make an undercut along the entire surface of the oval.

45 The carving is now complete.

Now undercut the inner facet of the second line **41** and then the outer facet of the first chip **42**. Repeat these steps along the other lines.

Finally, make cuts at the sides of the ovals anticlockwise, which are on the diagonal lines of the pattern **43**. Then make an undercut along the entire surface of the oval **44**.

Repeat the stages in all the sections. The carving is now complete **45**.

IMAGINARY TOWN

This pattern is completely filled with different chips with a different number of facets. There are no empty spaces without carving (except for the small 'drops').

TOOLS AND MATERIALS

- Basswood board (at least 100mm square, 1.5mm thick)

- 5mm mechanical pencil with H or HB (#3 or #2) lead

- Ruler

- Compass

- Skew knife

- Sandpaper or leather strips for sharpening

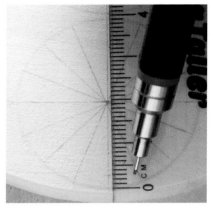

1 Mark a dot 3mm from the main circle of the pattern and draw another circle.

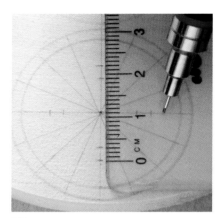

2 Mark two dots on the four perpendicular lines.

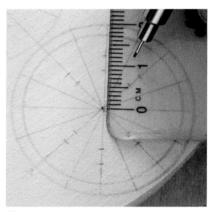

3 Mark two dots on the four diagonal lines.

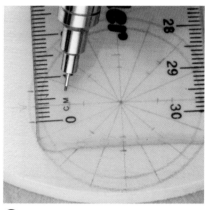

4 Mark dots on the main circle 3.5mm to the right and left of the perpendicular lines.

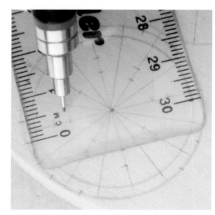

5 Mark dots on the main circle 2.5mm to the right and left of the diagonal lines.

DRAWING PROCESS

First prepare a main circle for the pattern. Using a compass, draw a circle with a radius of 2cm. Then draw two perpendicular lines that intersect at the centre and two diagonal lines that divide the quarters of the circle in half, forming eighths. Now divide the spaces in half again, so you have a circle with 16 identical triangles. Using a pencil and starting from the top of one of the perpendicular lines, mark each of the lines clockwise with numbers: 1, 2, 3. . .16. These marks will help when you are drawing the main pattern.

Mark a dot 3mm from the main circle of the pattern and, using a compass, draw a circle **1**.

Next, mark two sets of dots on the perpendicular lines: mark the first set of dots 1.1cm from the centre of the pattern, then mark the second set 8mm from the centre of the pattern **2**.

Next, mark two sets of dots on the diagonal lines: mark the first set of dots 1.25cm from the centre of the pattern, then the second set 9mm from the centre of the pattern **3**.

Mark dots on the main circle 3.5mm to the right and left of the perpendicular lines **4**. Then mark dots on the main circle 2.5mm to the right and left of the diagonal lines **5**.

Now mark dots 1mm to the right and left of the perpendicular lines between the dots that are 1.1cm and 8mm from the centre of the pattern **6** and then draw parallel lines **7**.

Next, draw a pair of curved lines to the right and left of a perpendicular line from the dot on the main circle next to the perpendicular line to the top of the short parallel line **8**. Then draw curved lines parallel to the previously drawn curved lines **9**. Connect the ends of the interior curved lines on the main circle with the points where the inner circle intersects the second curved lines **10**.

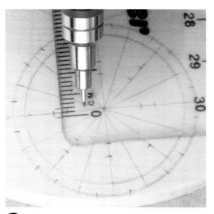

6 Mark a dot 1mm to the right and left of the perpendicular lines between the dots that are 1.1cm and 8mm from the centre of the pattern.

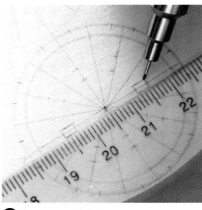

7 Draw parallel lines.

8 Draw a curved line to the right and left of a perpendicular line.

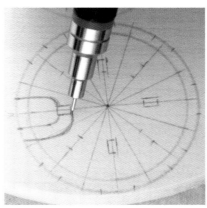

9 Draw a curved line that is parallel to the first curved line.

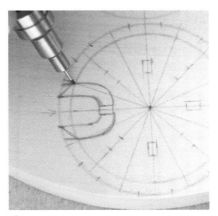

10 Connect the end of the interior curved lines on the main circle with the points where the inner circle intersects the second curved lines.

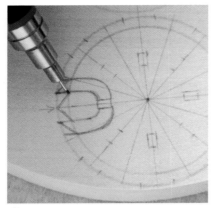

11 Draw lines connecting the end of a perpendicular line to the dots where the inner circle intersects the two interior curved lines.

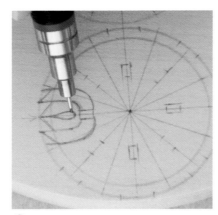

12 Draw two curved lines by hand inside the space to the right and left of the perpendicular line to form a drop.

Now connect the end of the perpendicular line to the points where the inner circle intersects the interior curved lines **11**. Then, on each side of the perpendicular line and inside the resulting space, draw two curved lines by hand, forming the shape of a drop **12**.

Measure a radius of 5.5mm from the centre of the pattern and draw a circle **13**. Then mark dots on this circle that are 1mm to the right and left of a diagonal line **14**. Draw a curved line from the ends of the short parallel lines to the resulting dots **15**.

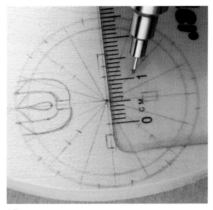

13 Measure a radius of 5.5mm from the centre of the pattern and draw a circle.

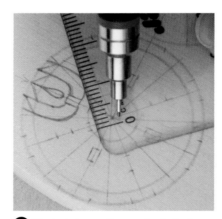

14 Mark dots on the central circle 1mm to the right and left of a diagonal line.

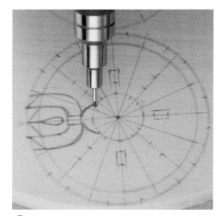

15 Draw a curved line connecting the ends of the short parallel lines to the dots on the central circle.

Connect the previously marked dots on the central circle to the centre of the pattern, drawing curved lines **16**.

Mark a dot 1mm from the outer line of the main figure of the pattern **17**. Then mark two dots 9mm from the centre of the pattern that are 1.5mm to the right and left of the nearby diagonal line **18**. Connect these two dots together by drawing a straight line **19**. Then draw a curved line parallel to the outer line of the main figure of the pattern, starting from the second circle **20**.

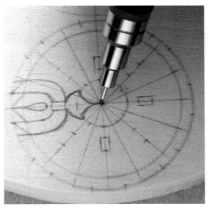

16 Connect the dots on the central circle to the centre of the pattern, drawing curved lines.

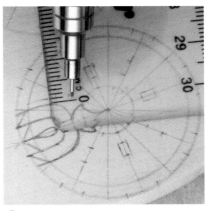

17 Mark a dot 1mm from the outer top side of the main figure.

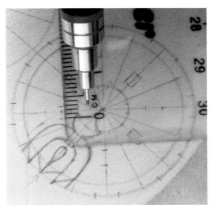

18 Mark two dots 9mm from the centre of the pattern that are 1.5mm to the right and left of the nearby diagonal line.

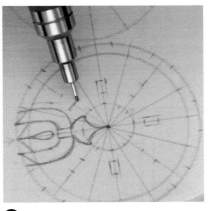

19 Connect these two dots together.

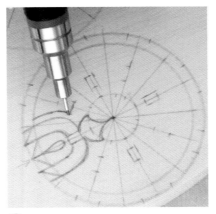

20 Draw a curved line parallel to the outer line of the main figure of the pattern to the short line.

21 Connect the dot next to the diagonal line on the outside circle to the end of the curved line.

22 From the previous dot on the main circle, draw a line parallel to diagonal line.

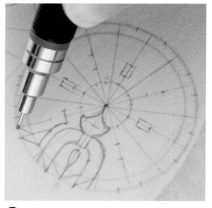

23 Connect the end of the diagonal line to the point where the second circle intersects the short line that is parallel to the diagonal line.

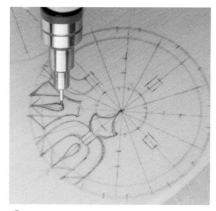

24 Draw two curved lines by hand in the space to the right and left of the diagonal line.

25 Draw two curved lines by hand inside each of the four ovals at the centre of the pattern.

26 Draw a line to the edge of the shape that is parallel to the outer curved line of the main figure, then repeat in the other sections.

Connect the dot that is next to the end of the diagonal line to the end of the previously drawn curved line **21**. Draw a line that is parallel to the diagonal line, starting from a dot on the main circle that is near the diagonal line **22**. Connect the end of the diagonal line to the point where the second circle intersects the short line that is parallel to the diagonal line **23**. Then draw two curved lines by hand inside the resulting space, to the right and left of the diagonal line, forming a drop shape **24**. Repeat these steps to fill the remaining quarters of the pattern.

Inside each of the ovals at the centre of the pattern, draw two curved lines by hand to the right and left of the diagonal line, forming an oval with sharp points **25**.

Draw a line to the edge that is parallel to the outer curved line of the main figure to form a rhombus with curved sides **26**. Repeat in the other sections. The pattern is now ready for carving.

CARVING PROCESS

Start working near the drop, first carving the rhombus with curved sides. Undercut the sides at an angle of about 60 degrees **27**, then cut the long and short sides of the straight-wall chip at an angle of about 90 degrees **28**. Next, undercut the short side of the chip at an angle of about 65 degrees **29**, and then cut the sides of the straight-wall chip on the other side **30**.

Start undercutting this complex chip by carving the straight-wall chips. If the chips go along the grain, start carving the chip where the grain changes direction. Undercut the chip first, for example, working away from yourself **31** and then finish undercutting working towards yourself **32** (or vice versa).

27 Undercut the sides of the rhombus at an angle of about 60 degrees.

28 Cut the long and short sides of the straight-wall chip.

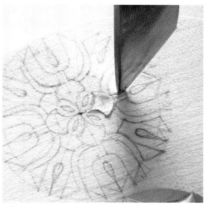

29 Undercut the short side of the chip at an angle of about 65 degrees.

30 Cut the sides of the straight-wall chip on the other side of the chip.

31 Undercut the chip, working away from yourself.

32 Finish undercutting the chip working towards yourself.

33 Cut the base of the drop.

34 Cut the short and long sides of the outer straight-wall chip.

Repeat these steps with another straight-wall chip but do not remove the tip of the knife from the wood. Change the angle of undercutting and make a cut at the base of the drop at an angle of about 60 degrees **33**. Repeat all the steps in undercutting if the chip does not pop out.

Next, cut the short and long sides of the outer straight-wall chip **34**, then carve the straight-wall chip with two undercuts **35**.

Now cut the short side of the straight-wall chip in the second main figure of the pattern **36**. Then make a cut on the long side of the straight-wall chip by leading the tip of the knife right to the curved line of the rhombus **37**.

35 Finish undercutting the outer straight-wall chip, working towards yourself.

36 Cut the short side of the straight-wall chip in the second main figure.

37 Make a cut on the long side of the straight-wall chip by leading the tip of the knife right to the curved line of the rhombus.

Make a cut perpendicular to the central ovals at the base of the complex chip at an angle of 60–65 degrees ❸❽. Then carve the sides of the second straight-wall chip in this chip and, without removing the tip of the knife from the wood, make a cut at the base of the drop in the second figure ❸❾. Repeat the steps in the carving if the chip does not pop out.

Cut the sides of the straight-wall chip between the two different drop figures ❹❶ and then carve it ❹❶.

Make a cut at an angle of about 65 degrees at the short side at the base of the six-sided chip between the two main figures of the pattern ❹❷. Then, using the tip of the knife, undercut the long facet ❹❸.

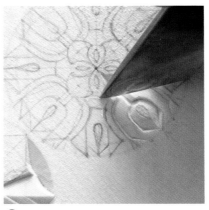
❸❽ Make a cut at the base of the chip perpendicular to the oval.

❸❾ Make a cut the base of the drop in the second figure.

❹❶ Cut the sides of the straight-wall chip between the two different drop figures.

❹❶ Carve the straight-wall chip.

❹❷ Make a cut at the short side of the base of the six-sided chip.

❹❸ Undercut the long facet, using the tip of the knife.

44 Cut the short side at the top of the six-sided chip at an angle of 45 degrees.

45 Cut the second short side of the six-sided chip.

Now cut the short side at the top of the six-sided chip at an angle of 45 degrees **44**. Change the grip of the knife in your hand and cut the second short side **45**. Then cut the second long curved edge **46**. Finish carving the six-sided chip with the facet at the top, using an angle of about 60 degrees **47**.

Next, using the tip of a knife, make a cut at the base of the side of the second main figure in the pattern **48**.

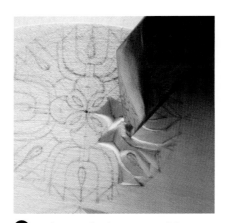

46 Undercut the long curved facet.

47 Finish carving the chip along the facet at the top, working at an angle of about 60 degrees.

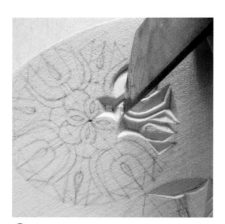

48 Make a cut at the base of the side of the second main figure in the pattern.

Carve the small ovals inside the central ovals at an angle of about 65 degrees 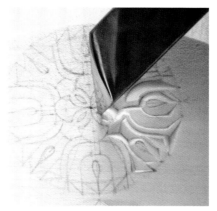. Then cut the facets around them. Start undercutting the sides from the inner facets at an angle of about 60 degrees, grabbing the base or side of the main shape with the tip of the knife ⑩. Change the grip of the knife in your hand and cut the outer sides ⑪. The first section of the pattern has been carved ⑫.

Repeat the steps to fill the remaining quarters of the pattern. The carving is now complete ⑬.

49 Carve the sides of the oval at an angle of about 65 degrees.

50 Undercut the inner facets at an angle of about 60 degrees.

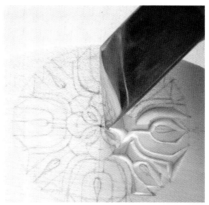

51 Cut the outer sides of the chip.

52 The first section of the pattern has been carved.

53 The carving is now complete.

SUNRAYS

This pattern, like the previous one, is almost completely filled with carving, but this time it is based not on sharp edges but on layering.

TOOLS AND MATERIALS

- Basswood board (at least 100mm square, 1.5mm thick)

- 5mm mechanical pencil with H or HB (#3 or #2) lead

- Ruler

- Compass

- Skew knife

- Sandpaper or leather strips for sharpening

1 Mark a dot 1.6cm from the centre of the pattern and draw a circle.

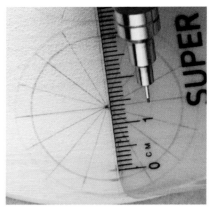

2 Measure a radius of 1.4cm from the centre of the pattern.

3 Draw curved lines between the straight lines to the right and left of the perpendicular lines.

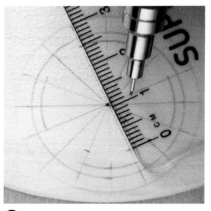

4 Mark a dot 1.1cm from the centre of the pattern on the lines to the right and left of the perpendicular lines.

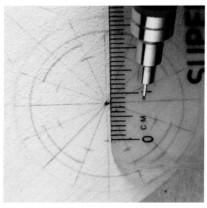

5 Mark a short line 8mm from the centre of the pattern on the diagonal lines.

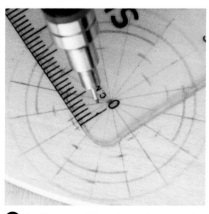

6 On the resulting short line, mark a dot 1mm to the right and left of the diagonal line.

DRAWING PROCESS

First prepare a main circle for the pattern. Using a compass, draw a circle with a radius of 2cm. Then draw two perpendicular lines that intersect at the centre and two diagonal lines that divide the quarters of the circle in half, forming eighths. Now divide the spaces in half again, so you have a circle with 16 identical triangles. Using a pencil and starting from the top of one of the perpendicular lines, mark each of the lines clockwise with numbers: 1, 2, 3. . .16. These marks will help when you are drawing the main pattern.

Mark a dot 1.6cm from the centre of the pattern and then draw a circle **1**.

Now mark a dot 1.4cm from the centre of the pattern on a perpendicular line **2** and then, using a compass, draw curved lines between the lines on the right and left of the perpendicular lines **3**.

Measure a radius of 1.1cm from the centre of the pattern **4** and, using a compass, mark the dots on the lines that are to the right and left of the perpendicular lines.

Next, mark a short line 8mm from the centre on the diagonal lines **5**. Mark dots on the resulting short lines that are 1mm to the right and left of the diagonal line **6**.

Then draw a thicker line to define the lines of the pattern. Start from a dot 1.4cm from the centre on a line next to a perpendicular line and draw it to a dot on the same line that is 1.1cm from the centre **7**. Then draw a line from the last dot to the dot next to the nearby diagonal line **8**. Now connect the last dot to the centre of the pattern **9**. Repeat the steps in reverse order to make a mirror image on the other side of the perpendicular line. Now repeat the steps to fill the remaining sections in the pattern.

Then measure a radius of 7.5mm from the centre of the pattern and, using a compass, draw short curved lines that intersect the perpendicular lines **10**.

Draw rhombuses inside the main figures of the pattern. To do so, first mark dots on the resulting curved lines 2.5mm to the right and left of the perpendicular lines **11**.

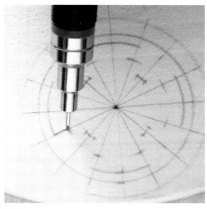

7 Draw a thicker line to define the lines of the pattern.

8 Draw a line from the dot that is on the line to the left of the perpendicular line to the dot that is next to the diagonal line of the pattern.

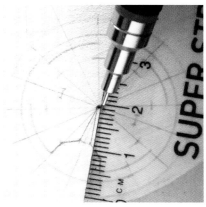

9 Connect the dot that is on the short line to the centre of the pattern.

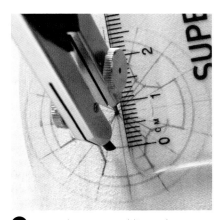

10 Draw short curved lines that intersect the perpendicular lines.

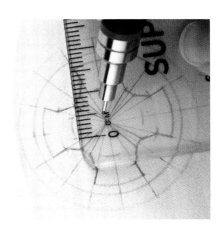

11 Mark dots on the curved lines that are 2.5mm to the right and left of the perpendicular lines.

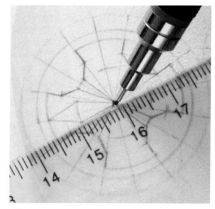

12 Draw lines from where a curved line meets a perpendicular line to the dots 7.5mm from the centre and then to the centre of the pattern.

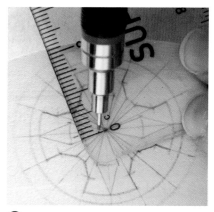

13 Mark a dot 1mm from the lines of the rhombus, then draw parallel lines inside it.

Draw lines from the point where the curved line intersects a perpendicular line to the dots on the curved line that are 7.5mm from the centre of the pattern and on the right and left of the perpendicular line. Then draw lines from the same two dots to the centre of the pattern **12**.

Mark a dot 1mm from the lines of the resulting rhombus and draw parallel lines inside it **13**. Now mark a dot 1mm from the lines of the main figure of the pattern **14** and also draw parallel lines inside it **15**.

Mark a dot on the main circle of the pattern 2mm to the right and left of a perpendicular line **16**.

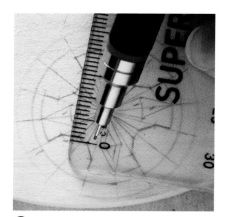

14 Mark a dot inside the main figure of the pattern 1mm from the lines.

15 Draw parallel lines.

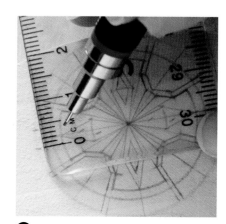

16 Mark a dot 2mm on the main circle to the right and left of a perpendicular line.

Connect the resulting dots to the point where the curved line intersects the perpendicular line 17.

Next, mark a dot that is 1.3cm from the centre of the pattern on a diagonal line 18. Mark a dot on the main circle of the pattern 3mm to the right and left of the diagonal line 19.

Draw straight lines that connect the resulting dots together 20. Next, connect the end of the diagonal line to the points where the inner circle of the pattern intersects the sides of the triangle 21.

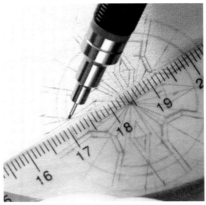

17 Connect the dots to the point where the curved line intersects the perpendicular line.

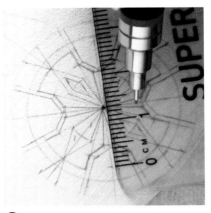

18 Mark a dot 1.3cm from the centre on a diagonal line.

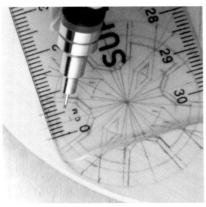

19 Mark dots on the main circle 3mm to the right and left of the diagonal line.

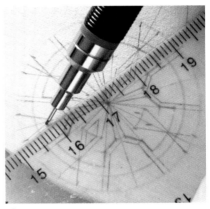

20 Draw straight lines to connect the dots together.

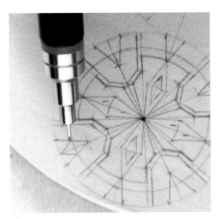

21 Draw lines from the end of the diagonal line to the points where the inner circle intersects the sides of the triangle.

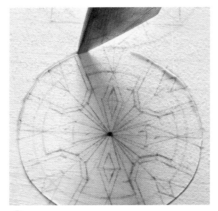

22 Cut the perimeter of the circle at an angle of about 90 degrees.

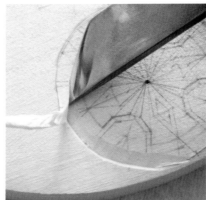
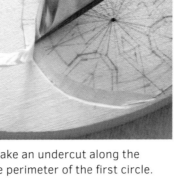

23 Make an undercut along the entire perimeter of the first circle.

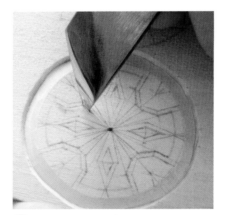

24 Start undercutting all the outside lines of the shape at an angle of about 60 degrees.

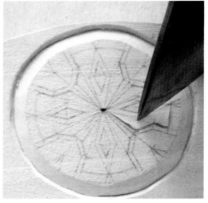

25 Finish carving the chip by undercutting the inside lines of the shape.

CARVING PROCESS

Begin to carve the pattern by cutting the perimeter of the circle, making cuts at an angle of about 90 degrees **22**.

Now place the knife on the circle 1.6cm from the centre of the pattern, near the perimeter, and, laying the knife close to the surface of the wood, make an undercut along the entire perimeter of the first circle **23**.

Next, remove the chip that surrounds the rhombus in the centre of the main figure of the pattern. First, undercut all the outer sides of the shape at an angle of about 60 degrees **24**. Then finish carving the chip by undercutting the inside lines of the shape **25**.

Redraw the lines that were removed when undercutting the space between the two outer circles at the perimeter **26**.

Carve the small rhombus that is inside the large rhombus at an angle of 60–65 degrees **27**. Now lay the knife close to the surface of the wood and make a cut along the entire top surface between the outer side of the small rhombus and the outer side of the large rhombus **28**.

Now draw two lines on the top surface, across the centre of the rhombus, where the two sides meet **29**. Make two cuts at these lines perpendicular to the surface of the wood **30**, and then two undercuts at an angle of about 65 degrees **31**.

26 Redraw the lines that were removed when undercutting the chip.

27 Carve the small rhombus at an angle of 60–65 degrees.

28 Make a cut along the entire top surface between the two rhombuses.

29 Draw two lines on the top surface, across the centre of the rhombus.

30 Make two cuts perpendicular to the surface of the wood.

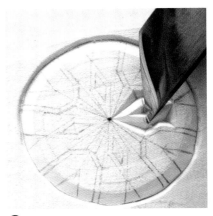

31 Make two undercuts at an angle of about 65 degrees.

32 Cut the base of the triangle at an angle of about 90 degrees.

33 Carve the sides of the triangle at an angle of about 45 degrees.

Next, carve the triangles at the perimeter of the pattern. First, cut the base of the triangle that is on the perpendicular line, in line with the carved rhombus, at an angle of about 90 degrees **32**. Carve the sides of the triangle at an angle of 45 degrees **33**.

Now undercut the base of the two small triangles inside the larger triangle on the nearby diagonal line at an angle of about 90 degrees **34**. Now carve the sides of these triangles at an angle of about 60 degrees **35**.

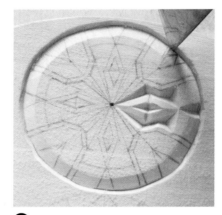

34 Undercut the bases of the two small triangles along the perimeter that are near the diagonal line.

35 Carve the sides of these small triangles at an angle of 60 degrees.

Carve the lines for the contour line carving, starting from the inner facets and leading the knife from the vertices of the small triangles to the point where two chips connect to each other **36**. Then undercut the outer facets of the chips **37**.

Cut the sides of the adjoining lines that go between the two main figures of the pattern at an angle of about 90 degrees **38**. Then undercut along the long line with a straight cut at an angle of about 65 degrees **39**.

36 Undercut the inner facets of the contour lines.

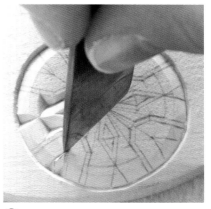

37 Undercut the outer facets of the two chips.

38 Cut along the adjoining lines between the two main figures at an angle of about 90 degrees.

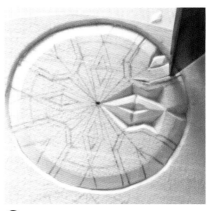

39 Undercut along the long line with a straight cut at an angle of about 65 degrees.

40 Carve the surface from the long side towards the short one.

41 Make a cut to level the surface.

Lay the knife close to the surface of the wood and carve the surface, moving from the long side to the short one **40**. Then make another cut to level the surface **41**.

Next, make a cut perpendicular to the surface of the wood along the diagonal line **42** and make two cuts at an angle of about 60 degrees **43**.

Make a cut starting from the main outside circle to the edge of the main figure at an angle of about 65 degrees **44**. Then make a second cut to finish the contour line carving **45**.

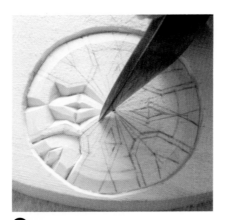

42 Make a cut perpendicular to the surface of the wood along the diagonal line.

43 Make two cuts at an angle of about 60 degrees.

44 Make a cut from the main circle to the edge of the main figure at an angle of about 65 degrees.

45 Now undercut the inner facet of the chip.

Cut one half of the surface along the perimeter of the main pattern, starting at the contour line carving **46**. Now make a cut between the two circles at the perimeter of the main pattern, cutting towards the outside edge **47**. Level the surface between these two circles with straight cuts **48**.

This section is almost complete, but first repeat the steps to fill the remaining quarters of the pattern. Finally, make rounded cuts between the inside circle at the perimeter and the edges of the main figures of the pattern, working towards the circle **49**.

The carving is now complete **50**.

46 Cut one half of the surface along the perimeter of the main pattern.

47 Make cuts between the two circles at the perimeter of the main pattern, working towards the outside.

48 Level the surfaces between the two circles by making straight cuts.

49 Make rounded cuts between the circle and the main figures.

50 The carving is now complete.

MAP IN THE SAND

This pattern consists of multi-level triangles connected to each other with thin four-sided chips, but the space between the two circles is larger than in previous patterns.

TOOLS AND MATERIALS

- Basswood board (at least 100mm square, 1.5mm thick)

- 5mm mechanical pencil with H or HB (#3 or #2) lead

- Ruler

- Compass

- Skew knife

- Sandpaper or leather strips for sharpening

1 Mark two dots from the centre of the pattern on any straight line and draw two circles.

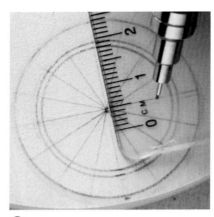

2 Mark a dot 5mm from the centre of the pattern on any straight line and draw a circle.

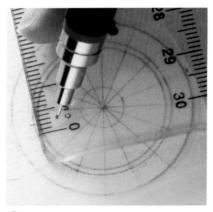

3 Divide the spaces between the straight lines in half and mark dots on the third circle of the pattern.

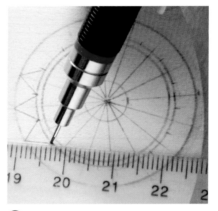

4 Draw lines between the ends of the straight lines and the dots on the third circle of the pattern.

DRAWING PROCESS: PART ONE

First prepare a main circle for the pattern. Using a compass, draw a circle with a radius of 2cm. Then draw two perpendicular lines that intersect at the centre and two diagonal lines that divide the quarters of the circle in half, forming eighths. Now divide the spaces in half again, so you have a circle with 16 identical triangles. Using a pencil and starting from the top of one of the perpendicular lines, mark each of the lines clockwise with numbers: 1, 2, 3. . .16. These marks will help when you are drawing the main pattern.

Mark two dots on any straight line: make the first dot 1.5cm from the centre of the pattern; make the second one 1.4cm from the centre **1**. Using a compass, draw two circles.

Also mark a dot 5mm from the centre of the pattern and draw a circle **2**.

Next, divide the spaces between straight lines in half and mark a dot on the third circle from the outside of the pattern **3**. Draw lines that connect the ends of the straight lines with the resulting dots **4**.

Now mark dots 1mm from the sides of the triangles clockwise, starting from the line that meets the top of line 1, then the line that meets the top of line 2, and so on. Draw parallel lines 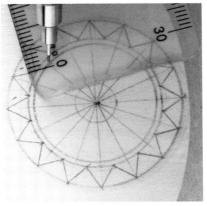 5 .

5 Mark a dot 1mm from one side of the triangles and draw parallel lines.

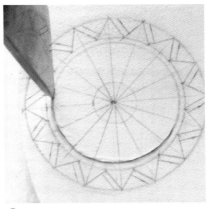

6 Make a cut along the perimeter of the second circle at an angle of about 90 degrees.

CARVING PROCESS: PART ONE

Before continuing with the drawing process, the centre of the pattern has to first be carved. To do this, cut the perimeter of the second circle that is 1.4cm from the centre of the pattern, at an angle of almost 90 degrees 6 .

Next, undercut the space between the central and second circles of the pattern (see box page 76). Lay the knife close to the surface of the wood and lead it confidently from the central circle towards the second circle to make a smooth surface. Work in sections, first undercutting two opposite areas, then moving on to the adjacent areas 7 .

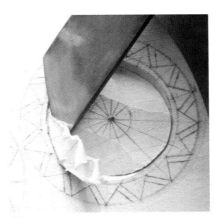

7 Carve the surface between the central and second circles.

8 Redraw the lines that were removed when carving the space.

9 Draw curved lines for the central pattern.

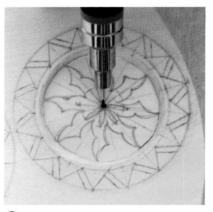

10 Draw two curved lines to the right and left of the lines inside the figures.

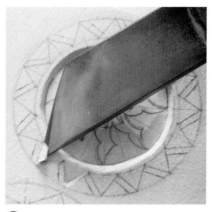

11 Carve the straight-wall chips where the base of the triangles are on the outside edge of the pattern.

12 Carve the straight-wall chips where the base of the triangles are along the first circle.

DRAWING PROCESS: PART TWO

Redraw the straight lines that were removed between the two circles when undercutting the space **8**.

Now draw curved lines by hand around the central circle, going clockwise. First, draw a curved line from the circle to the middle of the space between two lines. Then draw a line from the last point to the top of the second line. Next, draw a curved line from the top of the second line to the middle of the space to the right of that line, and then draw a curved line to the point where the circle intersects the third line. Repeat these steps in the remaining sections of the pattern **9**.

Draw two curved lines to the right and left of these straight lines, between the resulting dots and the centre of the pattern **10**. The pattern is now ready for carving.

CARVING PROCESS

Begin to carve the pattern at the straight-wall chips where the base of the triangles are along the main outside circle of the pattern **11**. Then carve the straight-wall chips where the base of the triangles are along the first interior circle that is 1.5cm from the centre of the pattern **12**.

Next, in the thin four-sided chips between the triangles, undercut the short sides at an angle of about 65 degrees, using the tip of a knife **13**. Then undercut the long sides of the chips **14**.

Make cuts for straight-wall chips clockwise inside the chips made along the first interior circle, about 1mm from the side **15**. Then turn the board and make cuts anticlockwise for straight-wall chips on the opposite side of the chips made along the main outside circle of the pattern **16**.

13 Cut the short sides of the thin four-sided chips at an angle of about 65 degrees, using the tip of a knife.

14 Undercut the long facets of the thin four-sided chips at an angle of about 65 degrees.

15 Carve a straight-wall chip inside the chips made along the first interior circle.

16 Carve a straight-wall chip inside the chips made along the main outside circle.

17 Carve the first outer facet of the first line along the grain, cutting at an angle of about 65 degrees.

18 Carve the second outer facet of the same line at an angle of about 65 degrees.

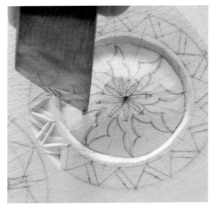

19 Undercut the first inner facet along the second line at an angle of about 65 degrees.

20 Undercut the second inner facet along the second line at an angle of about 65 degrees.

21 Cut the outer edge at the top of the chip, working away from yourself.

Carve the contour line carving, starting from the outer facet of a main figure that goes along the grain. Make the first cut in the outer facet closer to the centre of the pattern, cutting at an angle of about 65 degrees **17**. Then undercut the outer facet at the top of the shape **18**.

Change the grip of the knife in your hand and undercut the inner facet that connects to the previous line **19**. Then undercut the next facet by grabbing the previous facet with the tip of the knife **20**. Turn the board and start cutting the outer edge at the top of the chip, working away from yourself **21**.

Change the grip of the knife in your hand and cut the facet, working towards yourself ㉒. Undercut the next two facets, working towards yourself ㉓.

Finally, carve the central two-sided chips at an angle of about 60 degrees ㉔. Repeat the steps to fill in the remaining sections of the pattern.

The carving is now complete ㉕.

㉒ Cut the outer facet, working towards yourself.

㉓ Undercut the inner facet, working towards yourself.

㉔ Carve the central two-sided chips at an angle of about 60 degrees.

㉕ The carving is now complete.

AURORA

The pattern consists of different multi-level chips as well as a space between two circles.

TOOLS AND MATERIALS

- Basswood board (at least 100mm square, 1.5mm thick)

- 5mm mechanical pencil with H or HB (#3 or #2) lead

- Ruler

- Compass

- Skew knife

- Sandpaper or leather strips for sharpening

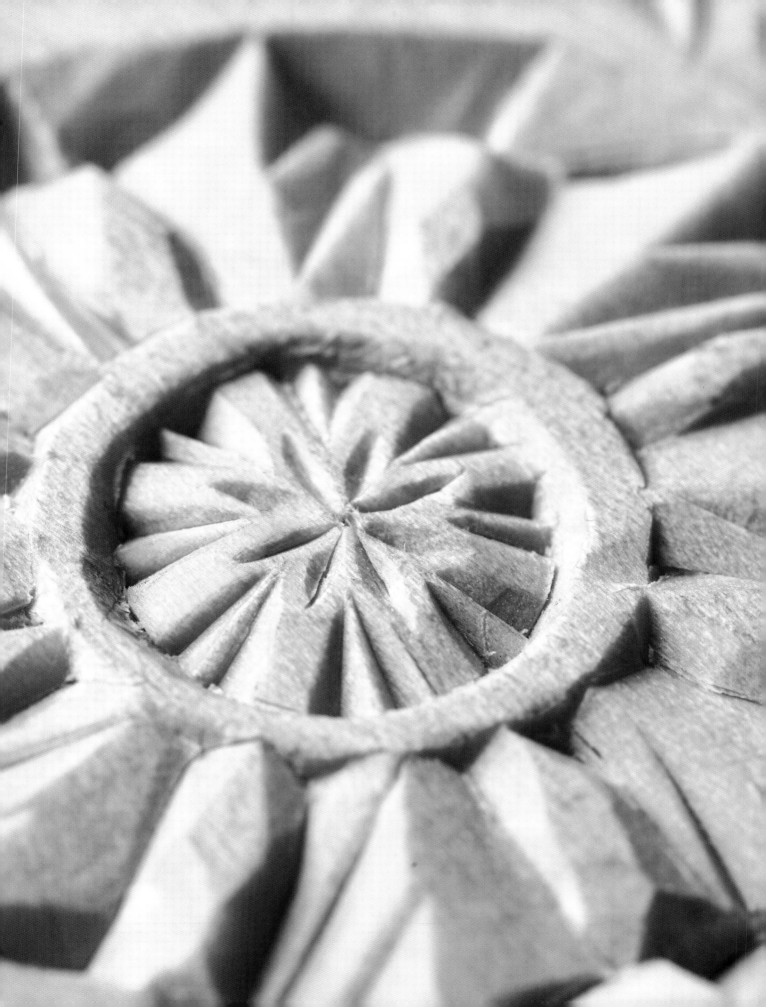

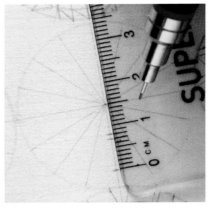

1 Mark three dots from the centre of the pattern on any straight line and draw three circles.

2 Mark two dots from the centre of the pattern and draw two circles.

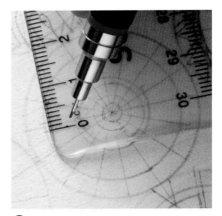

3 Starting at line 2, mark a dot 1mm to the right and left of every even-numbered line.

4 Draw two sets of parallel lines between the two outer pairs of cricles and the central circle.

5 Mark a dot that divides the thin space in half, then draw a short line.

DRAWING PROCESS

First prepare a main circle for the pattern. Using a compass, draw a circle with a radius of 2cm. Then draw two perpendicular lines that intersect at the centre and two diagonal lines that divide the quarters of the circle in half, forming eighths. Now divide the spaces in half again, so you have a circle with 16 identical triangles. Using a pencil and starting from the top of one of the perpendicular lines, mark each of the lines clockwise with numbers: 1, 2, 3. . .16. These marks will help you when you are drawing the main pattern.

Mark three dots on any straight line: make the first dot at 1.5cm from the centre of the pattern; the second one, 8mm from the centre; the third one, 7mm from the centre of the pattern **1**. Then, using a compass, draw three circles. Now make another two circles, marking one dot 5mm from the centre of the pattern and the second one, 3mm from the centre of the pattern **2**. Draw two circles.

Next, mark a dot 1mm to the right and left of every even-numbered straight line, starting from line 2 **3**. Then draw parallel lines between the outer pairs of circles and central circle as shown **4**. In the thin space between the top pairs of lines, divide the space in half and draw short lines at the marks **5**.

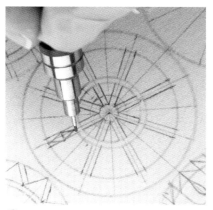

6 Now draw a rhombus inside the thin space.

7 Inside the two outer circles, draw lines from an odd-numbered line to the dots near the next two lines.

8 Cut the short central side of the straight-wall chip.

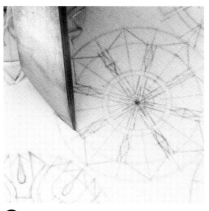

9 Cut the sides of the straight-wall chip.

10 Carve the straight-wall chip.

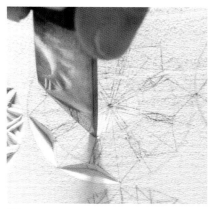

11 Cut the base of the figure to the right and then the left of the central line at an angle of about 90 degrees.

Draw a rhombus inside the thin space, with the four points where the two circles intersect the straight line and where the short line bisects the thin space **6**. Repeat these steps inside the remaining thin spaces.

Starting from line 3, between the two outer circles, connect the top of every odd-numbered line with the dots on the nearby circle to the right and left of the even-numbered lines **7**. The pattern is now ready for carving.

CARVING PROCESS

Start carving the pattern at the four-sided straight-wall chips where the bases are on the perimeter of the main circle. Undercut the short central side at an angle of about 90 degrees **8**, then the two sides **9**. Now carve the straight-wall chip **10**.

Cut the base of the five-sided main figure of the pattern, cutting to the right and then the left of the central line at an angle of about 90 degrees **11**.

12 Make a cut at an angle of 90 degrees along each side of the figure.

13 Make un undercut to left of the central line, then make another one to the right.

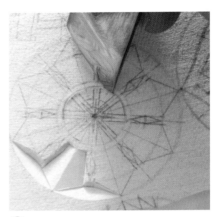

14 Make a cut along the perimeter of the third circle from the centre at an angle of about 90 degrees.

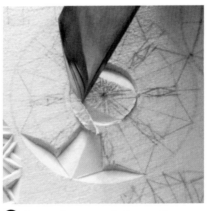

15 Carve the space between the second and third circles from the centre of the pattern.

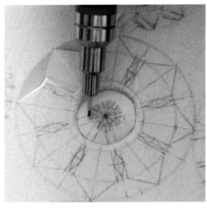

16 Redraw the lines that were removed when undercutting the surface between the circles.

Changing the angle for undercutting a chip

For chips of a standard size, the basic angles for undercutting facets will produce carved chips that look the best.

However, if you reduce the chips in size, the cutting angles will have to 'automatically' increase so that there is no chipping. That is, the smaller the chip, the greater the undercutting angle will need to be.

Make a cut along the side of the figure also at an angle of 90 degrees **12**. Lay the knife close to the surface of the wood and make two undercuts to the right and left of the central line **13**.

Next, make a cut along the perimeter of the third circle from the centre of the pattern at an angle of about 90 degrees **14**. Carve the space between the second and third circles from the centre of the pattern **15**. Then redraw the lines that were removed when undercutting the space between the circles **16**.

17 Undercut the bases of the triangles with the tip of a knife.

18 Now undercut the sides of the two triangles.

19 Make a cut at the top of the main figure.

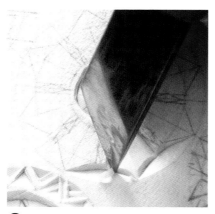

20 Make a curved undercut along the side.

21 Make a cut from the top right corner of the figure to the base of the central line.

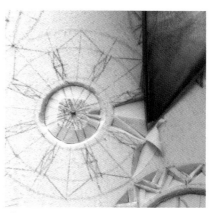

22 Lay the knife close to the surface of the wood and then undercut the surface.

In the redrawn central area, in the spaces between the parallel lines, carve two triangles by eye. Using the tip of the knife, undercut the bases of the triangles along the perimeter of the third circle from the centre **17**. Then undercut the sides of the triangles at an angle of 60–65 degrees **18**.

Next, make a cut at the top of the main five-sided figure **19** and then make a curved undercut along the side at an angle of 60–65 degrees **20**.

Now make a cut on the right side of the five-sided figure that goes from the top right corner of the figure to the base of the central line **21**. Lay the knife close to the surface of the wood and make a cut following the grain direction as for carving the base of a straight-wall chip **22**.

23 Make a cut about 2mm from the previous cut.

24 Make a cut perpendicular to the base of the straight-wall chip.

25 Undercut the part of the base on the multi-level side of the five-sided figure.

26 Make a cut at the base of the thin space next to the five-sided figure.

27 Undercut the wood along the side of the rhombus.

28 Make an undercut along the side of the rhombus at the top of the thin space.

Make a parallel cut about 2mm from the previous cut **23** and undercut the surface. Make a cut perpendicular to the base of the straight-wall chip that divides the base of the chip in half **24**. Then undercut the part of the base on the multi-level side of the five-sided figure **25**.

Next, make a cut at the base of the thin space with a rhombus **26**, then undercut the wood along the side of the rhombus **27**. Now make one more undercut along the side of the rhombus but at the top of the thin space **28**.

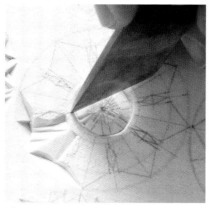

29 Make a cut at the base of the multi-level side of the five-sided figure right under the rhombus.

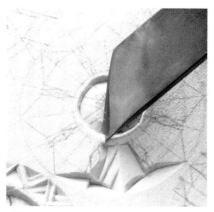

30 Make an undercut that starts from the sharp edge of the figure.

31 Draw ovals in the spaces between the parallel lines.

32 Carve the two-sided chips at an angle of about 65 degrees.

33 The carving is now complete.

Make a cut at the base of the multi-level side of the five-sided figure right under the rhombus **29** and make an undercut that starts from the sharp edge of the five-sided figure **30**.

Finally, draw ovals in the spaces between the parallel lines that start from the centre of the pattern and end at the second circle of the pattern **31**. Now carve the resulting two-sided chips at an angle of about 65 degrees **32**. Repeat the steps to fill in the remaining sections of the pattern.

The carving is now complete **33**.

INSIDE A DEWDROP

The complexity of the carving of the last pattern, like one of the previous patterns, lies in the sequence of steps that you need to make to move from one chip to the next. This pattern combines everything you have learned in the previous projects.

TOOLS AND MATERIALS

- Basswood board (at least 100mm square, 1.5mm thick)

- 5mm mechanical pencil with H or HB (#3 or #2) lead

- Ruler

- Compass

- Skew knife

- Sandpaper or leather strips for sharpening

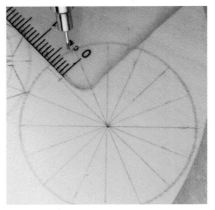

1 Mark 4mm from the main circle on line 2.

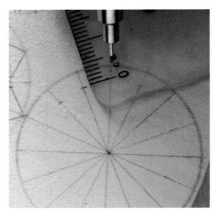

2 Mark 4mm from the main circle on line 3.

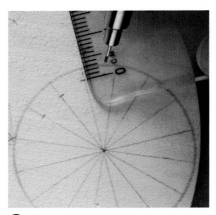

3 Mark 3mm from the main circle on line 4.

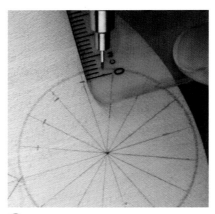

4 Mark 2mm from the main circle on line 5.

5 Mark 1mm from the main circle on line 6.

6 Connect the dots by drawing a curved line, starting with line 1 and ending on line 7.

DRAWING PROCESS

First prepare a main circle for the pattern. Using a compass, draw a circle with a radius of 2cm. Then draw two perpendicular lines that intersect at the centre and two diagonal lines that divide the quarters of the circle in half, forming eighths. Now divide the spaces in half again, so you have a circle with 16 identical triangles. Using a pencil and starting from the top of one of the perpendicular lines, mark each of the lines clockwise with numbers: 1, 2, 3. . .16. These marks will help when you are drawing the main pattern.

Mark five dots: make the first dot 4mm from the main circle on line 2 **1**; the second one, 4mm from the main circle on line 3 **2**; the third one, 3mm from the main circle on line 4 **3**; the fourth one, 2mm from the main circle on line 5 **4**; and the fifth one, 1mm from the main circle on line 6 **5**. Then connect the resulting dots by drawing a curved line **6** that begins on the main circle at line 1 and ends on the circle at line 7.

Now repeat these steps to make a mirrored curved line: make dots at 4mm on line 16, at 3mm on lines 15 and 14, at 2mm on line 13 and 1mm on line 12, then draw the curved line starting at line 1 and ending on line 11.

Next, start marking six dots for the central pattern: make the first dot 1.3cm from the centre of the pattern on line 14 **7**; the second one, 1.2cm from the centre on line 13 **8**; the third one, 1.2cm from the centre on line 12 **9**; the fourth one, 1.3cm from the centre on line 11 **10**; the fifth one, 1.4cm from the centre on line 10 **11**; and the sixth one, 1.6cm from the centre on line 9 **12**.

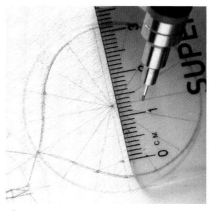

7 Mark a dot 1.3cm from the centre of the pattern on line 14.

8 Mark a dot 1.2cm from the centre of the pattern on line 13.

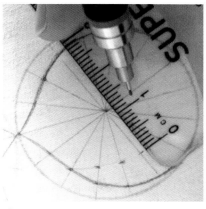

9 Mark a dot 1.2cm from the centre of the pattern on line 12.

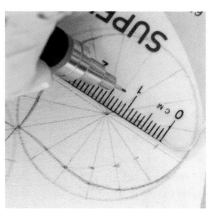

10 Mark a dot 1.3cm from the centre of the pattern on line 11.

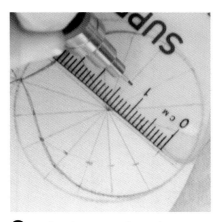

11 Mark a dot 1.4cm from the centre of the pattern on line 10.

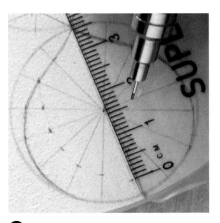

12 Mark a dot 1.6cm from the centre of the pattern on line 9.

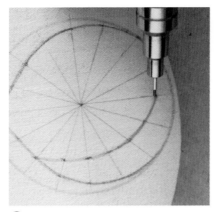

13 Connect the dots by drawing a curved line.

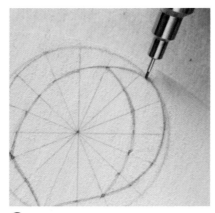

14 Repeat the steps of marking the dots to make the fourth curved line inside the circle.

Now connect the resulting dots with a curved line **13**.

Repeat these steps on the other side of the pattern to make a mirrored curved line: make dots 1.3cm from the centre on line 4; 1.2cm from the centre on line 5; 1.3cm from the centre on line 6; 1.3cm from the centre on line 7; 1.4cm from the centre on line 8; then draw a curved line, meeting the opposite curve on line 9 and smoothly ending it on the main circle at line 10 **14**.

For the next curve, mark eight dots: make the first dot 4mm from the outside circle on line 1 **15**; the second one, 1.3cm from the outside circle on line 16 **16**; and the third, 1.15cm from the outside circle on line 15 **17**.

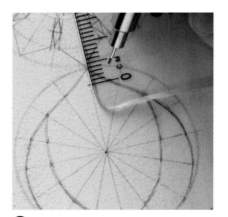

15 Mark 4mm from the main circle on line 1.

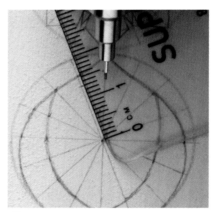

16 Mark a dot 1.3cm from a centre of the pattern on line 16.

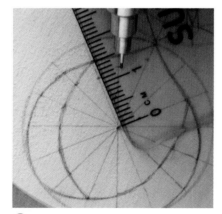

17 Mark a dot 1.15cm from a centre of the pattern on line 15.

Continue with the fourth dot at 1.05cm from the outside circle on line 14 **18**; the fifth one, 1cm from the outside circle on line 13 **19**; the sixth one, 1cm from the outside circle on line 12 **20**; the seventh one, 1.1cm from the outside circle on line 11 **21**; and the eighth one, 1.2cm from the outside circle on line 10 **22**. Now connect these dots by drawing a curved line.

Again, repeat the steps to make a mirrored curved line: make the first dot 1.3cm from the outside circle on line 2; 1.15cm from the outside circle on line 3; 1.05cm from the outside circle on line 4; 1cm from the outside circle on line 5; 1cm from the outside circle on line 6; 1.1cm from the outside circle on line 7; and 1.2cm from the outside circle on line 8. Starting at the end of the previously drawn curve on line 1 draw a curved line to the dot on line 8.

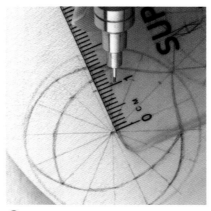

18 Mark a dot 1.05cm from a centre of the pattern on line 14.

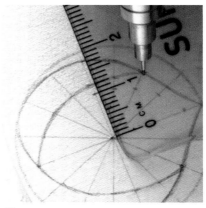

19 Mark a dot 1cm from a centre of the pattern on line 13.

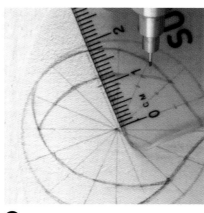

20 Mark a dot 1cm from a centre of the pattern on line 12.

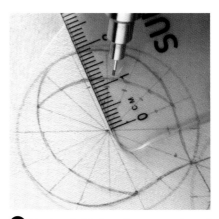

21 Mark a dot 1.1cm from a centre of the pattern on line 11.

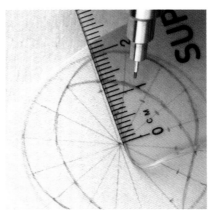

22 Mark a dot 1.2cm from a centre of the pattern on line 10.

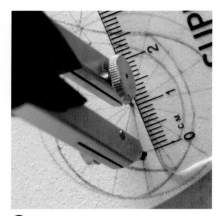

23 Measure a radius of 1.1cm from the centre of the pattern and draw two short lines between lines 8 and 9 and between lines 9 and 10.

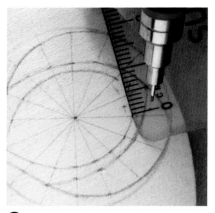

24 Divide the space between lines 8 and 9 and between lines 9 and 10 in half and mark dots on the short lines.

Draw two short lines 1.1cm from the centre of the pattern, one between lines 8 and 9 and the other between lines 9 and 10 **23**. Divide the space between these lines in half and mark the dots on the short lines **24**. Now connect the dot on line 10 to the dot between lines 9 and 10 **25**, and then draw a line from it to the point on line 9 where the sides of the two 'leaves' meet with each other **26**. Repeat the steps, connecting the dot on line 8 to the dot between lines 8 and 9, then to the point on line 9.

Mark a dot 9mm from the centre of the pattern on line 9 **27**. Now measure a radius of 1.3cm and, using a compass, draw a short line that intersects line 9 **28**.

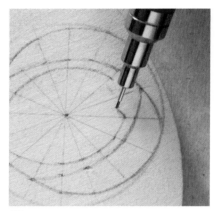

25 Connect the dot on line 10 with the dot between lines 9 and 10.

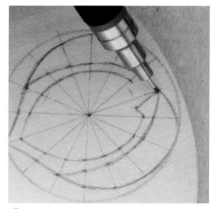

26 Connect the dot between lines 9 and 10 where the point and the sides of the two leaves meet.

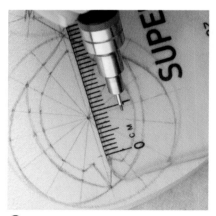

27 Mark a dot 9mm from the centre on line 9.

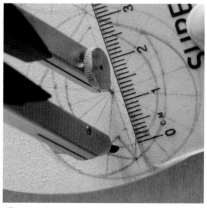

28 Measure a radius of 1.3cm and, using a compass, draw a short line that intersects line 9.

Now draw two lines to connect the lower dot on line 9 with the intersection line above it **29**.

Next, mark eight dots for the next curved line. Make the first dot 3mm from the top of the inner curved line on the left curved line of the central pattern between lines 16 and 1 **30**. Now measure from the centre of the pattern: make the second dot 9mm from the centre on line 16 **31**; the third one, 5mm from the centre of the pattern on line 15 **32**; and the fourth one, 4mm from the centre of the pattern on line 14 **33**.

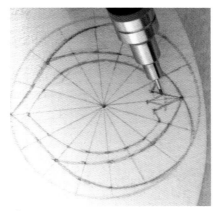

29 Connect the dot on line 9 to the points where the short line intersects the two lines in the central pattern.

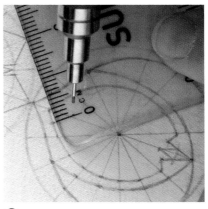

30 Mark a dot 3mm from the top of the central pattern on the left curved line of the central pattern.

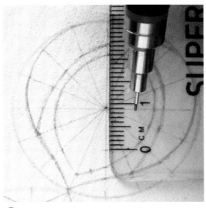

31 Mark a dot 9mm from the centre of the pattern on line 16.

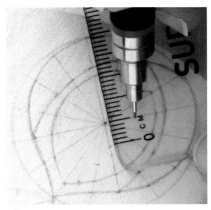

32 Mark a dot 5mm from the centre of the pattern on line 15.

33 Mark a dot 4mm from the centre of the pattern on line 14.

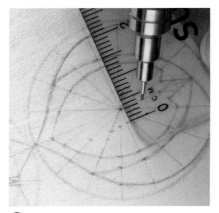

34 Mark a dot 3mm from the centre on line 13.

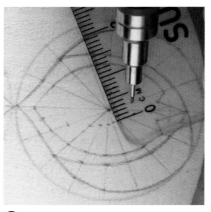

35 Mark a dot 3mm from the centre on line 12.

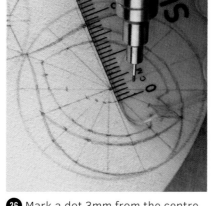

36 Mark a dot 3mm from the centre on line 11.

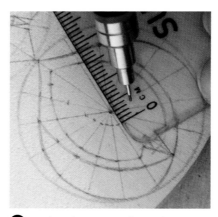

37 Mark a dot 3.5mm from the centre on line 10.

Continue with the fifth dot, marking it 3mm from the centre on line 13 **34**; the sixth one, 3mm from the centre on the line 12 **35**; the seventh one, 3mm from the centre on line 11 **36**; and the eighth one, 3.5mm from the centre on line 10 **37**. Now connect the resulting dots by drawing a curved line **38**.

Make another mirrored curved line: mark the first dot 3mm from the top of the inner curved line on the left curved line of the central pattern between lines 1 and 2. Then make the second dot 9mm from the centre on line 2; the third one, 5mm from the centre on line 3; the fourth one, 4mm from the centre on line 4; the fifth dot, 3mm from the centre on line 5; the sixth one, 3mm from the centre on the line 6; the seventh one, 3mm from the centre on line 7; and the eighth one, 3.5mm from the centre on line 8. Now draw a curved line.

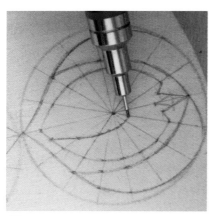

38 Connect the dots by drawing a curved line, then repeat to draw a curve on the other side.

Mark a dot 4mm from the top of the lines for the central pattern on line 1 **39**. Then draw two lines to it from the top of the nearby lines **40**.

From the top of the same central pattern lines in step 40, measure 5mm along the lines and make dots **41**.

Next, mark six dots: make the first dot 8.5mm from the centre of the pattern on line 15 **42**; the second one, 7mm from the centre on line 14 **43**; and the third one, 6.5mm from the centre on line 13 **44**.

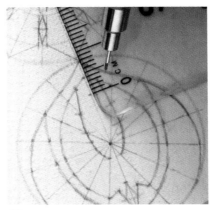

39 Mark a dot 4mm from the top of the central pattern on line 1.

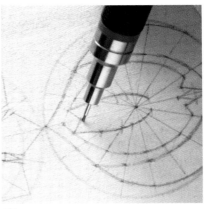

40 Connect the top of the lines of the central pattern with the dot on line 1.

41 Mark a dot 5mm from the end of the left line of the central pattern and also on the right line of the central pattern.

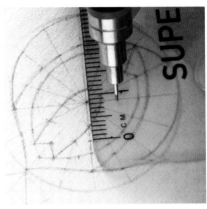

42 Mark a dot 8.5mm from the centre on line 15.

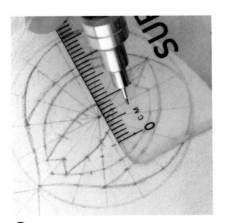

43 Mark a dot 7mm from the centre on line 14.

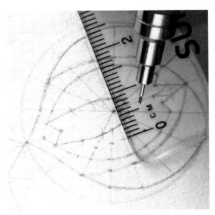

44 Mark a dot 6.5mm from the centre on line 13.

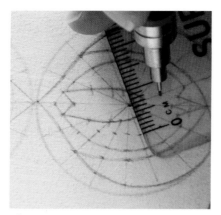

45 Mark a dot 7mm from the centre on line 12.

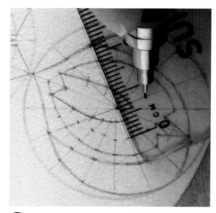

46 Mark a dot 7mm from the centre on line 11.

Continue with the fourth dot, 7mm from the centre of the pattern on line 12 **45**; the fifth one, 7mm from the centre on line 11 **46**; and the sixth, 8mm from the centre on line 10 **47**.

Now mark two dots 8mm from the centre of the pattern in the spaces between lines 8 and 9 and between lines 9 and 10 **48**.

Then, using a ruler, connect the two dots with broken lines, ending them 1mm on the right and on the left of line 9 **49**. Now connect the previously prepared dots by drawing a curved line, ending it at a broken line **50**.

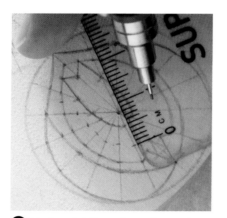

47 Mark a dot 8mm from the centre on line 10.

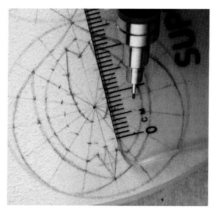

48 Mark two dots 8mm from the centre in the spaces between lines 8 and 9 and between lines 9 and 10.

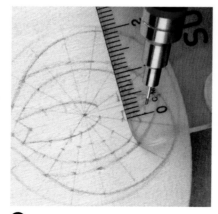

49 Using a ruler, begin to connect the dots with broken lines.

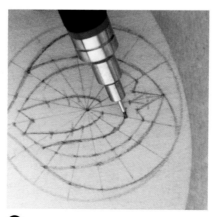

50 Now connect the dots by drawing a curved line, joining it with the broken line.

Connect the second dot on line 16 in the central pattern with the point where the previously drawn curved line began 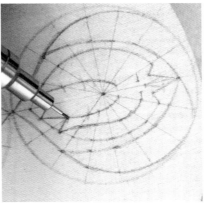.

Mark a dot 4mm from the centre of the pattern on line 9 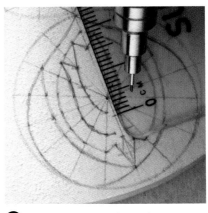 and draw a line to connect it with the end of the broken line ⑤③.

Repeat steps 42–47 to make a mirrored shape, starting with the first dot at 8.5mm from the centre on line 2; the second one, 7mm from the centre on line 3; the third one, 6.5mm from the centre on line 4; the fourth one, 7mm from the centre on line 5; the fifth one, 7mm from the centre on line 6; and the sixth one, 8mm from the centre on line 7. Draw similar lines as in steps 50–53.

Next, mark a short line 6mm from the centre of the pattern on line 1 ⑤④. Then measure 1.5mm to the right and left of line 1 at the resulting short line ⑤⑤. Draw by hand two curved lines that form an oval with sharp points: from the centre of the pattern, draw the line to the dot on the left of the short line and then to the third dot from the outside main circle. Repeat on the other side ⑤⑥.

51 Draw a line from the second dot on line 16 in the central pattern with the end of the previously drawn line.

52 Mark a dot 4mm from the centre of the pattern on line 9.

53 Connect the dot on line 9 with the ends of the broken lines.

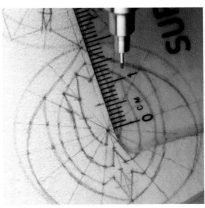

54 Mark a short line 6mm from the centre on line 1.

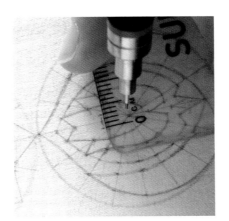

55 Measure 1.5mm to the right and left of line 1 at the short line.

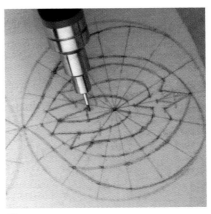

56 Draw by hand two curved lines that form an oval with sharp points.

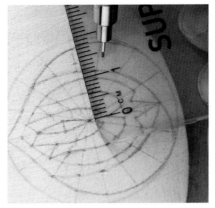

57 Mark a dot 1.4cm from the centre of the pattern on line 5.

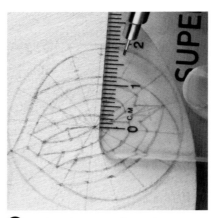

58 Mark a dot 1.7cm from the centre of the pattern on line 6.

The next stage is to draw the 'petals', which are at the base of the pattern. Mark the first two dots: make one dot 1.4cm from the centre of the pattern on line 5 **57**; the second one, 1.7cm from the centre on line 6 **58**. Start connecting these dots from the point where the line of the central pattern intersects line 4 and continuing to the next curved line between lines 6 and 7 **59**.

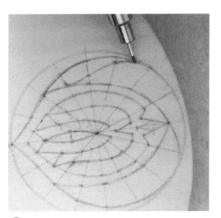

59 Connect the dots by drawing a curved line.

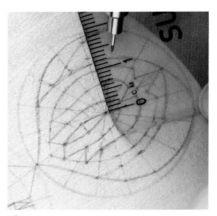

60 Mark a dot 1.3cm from the centre on line 6.

Mark another two dots: the first one, 1.3cm from the centre on line 6 **60**; the second one, 1.9cm from the centre on line 7 **61**. Start connecting the resulting dots from that point where the line of the central pattern intersects line 5 **62** and continuing to the curved line between lines 7 and 8.

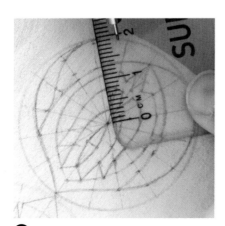

61 Mark a dot 1.9cm from the centre on line 7.

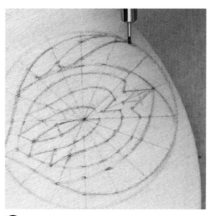

62 Connect the dots by drawing a curved line.

Mark a dot 1.5cm from the centre of the pattern on line 7 **63** and then draw a curved line from the point where the central pattern intersects line 6 and continue to the outside circle **64**.

Mark a dot 1.7cm from the centre of the pattern on line 8 **65** and draw a curved line from the dot where the central pattern intersects line 7 **66**. Do not mark a dot for the next leaf, but draw a curved line by hand between lines 8 and number 9, following the contours of the previously drawn petals **67**.

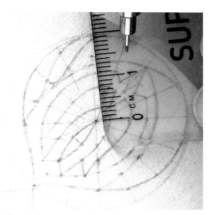

63 Mark a dot 1.5cm from the centre on line 7.

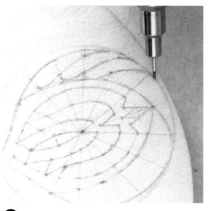

64 Draw a curved line starting at line 6 and through the dot on line 7 to the main outside circle.

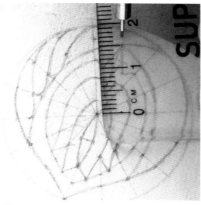

65 Mark a dot 1.7cm from the centre on line 8.

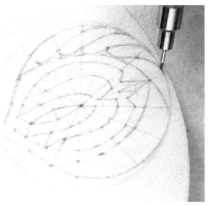

66 Draw a curved line from the dot where the central pattern intersects line 7 to the main outside circle.

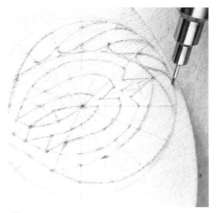

67 Draw a curved line between lines 8 and 9 that follows the contours of the previous petals.

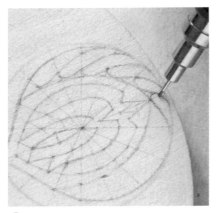

68 Round off the top of the last petal in the shape.

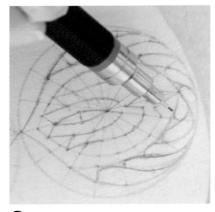

69 Repeat these steps to draw the petals on the left side of the pattern.

70 For the outer chips of the central pattern, highlight the tops on lines 4 and 14 with a thicker line.

71 Undercut the first short side at the base of the central pattern at an angle of about 60 degrees.

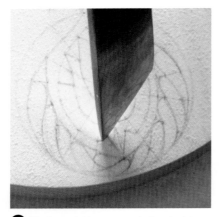

72 Undercut the second short side at the base of the central pattern at an angle of about 60 degrees.

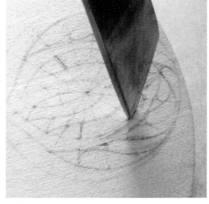

73 Undercut the lower part of the long side of the central pattern, working towards yourself.

Round off the top of the last petal in this shape **68**. Repeat these steps to draw the petals on the left side **69**.

Finally, draw the thicker lines on lines 4 and 14 on the outer chips of the central pattern to define the tops, where the cut will go **70**. The pattern is now ready for carving.

CARVING PROCESS

Start carving the pattern at the six-sided chip that is alongside the petals and goes around the central pattern.

First, undercut one of the short sides at the base of the pattern at an angle of about 60 degrees **71**, then, without changing the grip in your hand, undercut the second short side **72**.

Since the pattern goes along the grain, divide the long curved side in half by eye, and cut one part, working towards yourself **73**.

Now finish undercutting the side, working away from yourself, leading the knife to the top of the pattern **74**.

When the carving of the inner facets has been carved, start undercutting the outer ones. Lead the knife to the most curved point **75**, then turn the knife in your hand and finish undercutting the long side **76**.

Next, carve the two-sided chips that go around almost the entire perimeter of the circle. Undercut the side that partially connects to the previously carved six-sided chip at an angle of almost 90 degrees **77**, then cut the other side as if carving a base for a straight-wall chip **78**. (On this side, at the final stage of the carving, you will draw and carve small triangles or stars.)

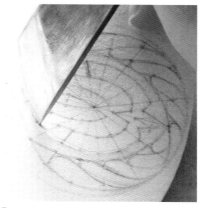

74 Undercut the top part of the long side, working away from youself.

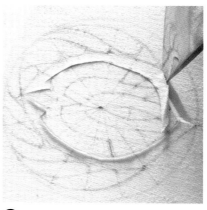

75 Start undercutting the outer facets of the six-sided chip.

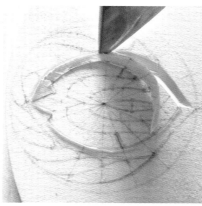

76 Finish undercutting the central six-sided chip.

77 Undercut the inner side of the two-sided chip at the perimeter at an angle of about 90 degrees.

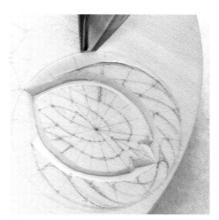

78 Lay the knife close to the wood surface and undercut the outer side of the two-sided chip, following the grain direction.

79 Cut the side of the first triangular straight-wall chip in the central pattern.

80 Carve the first straight-wall chip following the grain direction.

The central pattern consists of almost only the same straight-wall chips of different shapes. Start carving the first straight-wall chip in the shape of a triangle 79 and then undercut it following the grain direction 80. Then carve the straight-wall chip next to it 81. These are preparatory straight-wall chips, which will make it possible to cut the next long slightly curved straight-wall chips.

Make a cut at the short base side of the outer straight-wall chip 82 and then at the long side, both at at an angle of about 80 degrees 83. Lay the knife close to the wood surface and undercut the chip 84. If the knife stops going smoothly along the grain while undercutting the side, you may need to change the grip in your hand.

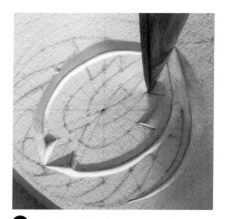

81 Cut the side of the second triangular straight-wall chip in the central pattern.

82 Cut the short base of the outer straight-wall chip in the central pattern.

83 Cut the long side of the outer straight-wall chip at an angle of 80–85 degrees.

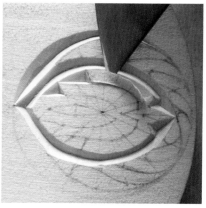

84 Lay the knife close to the wood and finish carving the first long straight-wall chip.

Now carve the next long straight-wall chip **85** and the last one, again at angles of about 80 degrees **86**.

Go back to the first long straight-wall chip and start cutting a multi-level triangle with a rhombus inside of it. To do this, place a knife about 2mm from the base and make a cut **87**, then make another cut that forms a triangle **88**. Now carve the straight-wall chip **89**. Next, draw two lines inside the chip by hand that form a rhombus **90** and carve two more straight-wall chips.

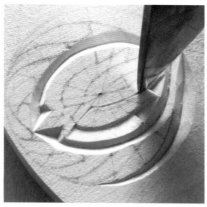

85 Cut the sides of the second long straight-wall chip at an angle of 80–85 degrees.

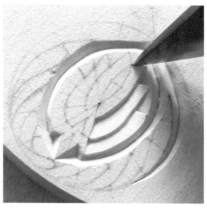

86 Cut the sides of the third long straight-wall chip at an angle of 80–85 degrees.

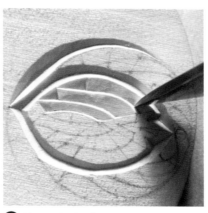

87 Place the knife 2mm from the base of the chip and make a cut.

88 Make one more cut, forming a triangle.

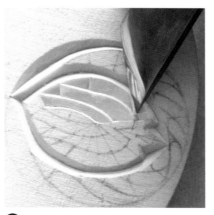

89 Undercut the straight-wall chip.

90 Draw two lines inside the straight-wall chip to form a rhombus.

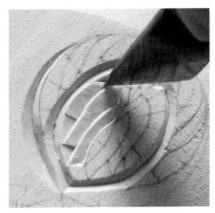

91 Make a cut with the tip of the knife at the side of the multi-level chip.

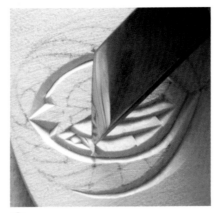

92 Finish carving the chip with a rounded undercut.

To finish the carving in the first long straight-wall chip, make a straight cut with the tip of the knife at the side of the chip you just carved **91**. Then turn the board and make a rounded undercut **92**.

Now start carving a multi-level triangle inside the second long straight-wall chip. Place the knife 2–3mm from the base of the chip and make a cut **93** and then make another cut to form a triangle **94**. Draw two lines next to it to form a rhombus inside the chip, and then carve two straight-wall chips **95**. Make a cut at the outer side of the multi-level chip, change the grip of the knife in your hand and make a rounded cut **96**.

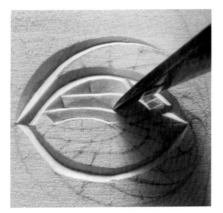

93 Place a knife 2–3mm from the base of the chip and make a cut.

94 Make one more cut, forming a triangle.

95 Carve two more straight-wall chips inside the chip.

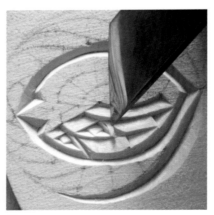

96 Finish carving the chip with a rounded undercut.

Next, carve a multi-level triangle inside the third long straight-wall chip. Place the knife 7–8mm from the base of the chip and make a cut 🟢97, then make another cut that forms a triangle 🟢98. Draw two lines to form a rhombus inside the chip, and then carve two straight-wall chips 🟢99. Make a cut on the outer side of the multi-level triangle, change the grip of the knife in your hand and make a rounded cut 🟢100.

Now make a cut in the middle of the first straight-wall chip 🟢101. Then make two undercuts at an angle of about 60 degrees 🟢102.

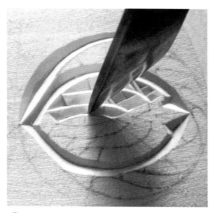

🟢97 Place the knife 7–8mm from the base of the chip and make a cut.

🟢98 Make one more cut, forming a triangle.

🟢99 Carve two more straight-wall chips inside the chip.

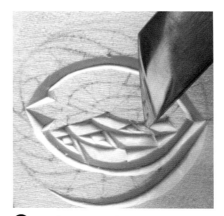

🟢100 Finish carving the chip with a rounded undercut.

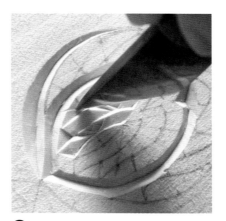

🟢101 Make a cut in the middle of the first straight-wall chip.

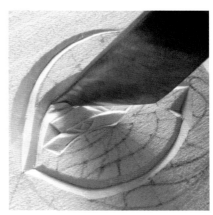

🟢102 Make two undercuts at an angle of about 60 degrees.

103 Make a cut in the middle of the second straight-wall chip.

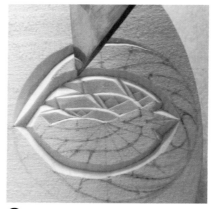

104 Make a straight cut at the top of the first petal at an angle of about 60 degrees.

Repeat these steps in a second straight-wall chip **103**.

Now begin carving the outer part of the pattern with the petals. Undercut the top of the first petal with a straight cut at an angle of about 60 degrees **104**. Then make a second undercut that follows the shape of the dewdrop **105**.

Next, make the first cut at the top of the second petal **106** and then the second undercut **107**.

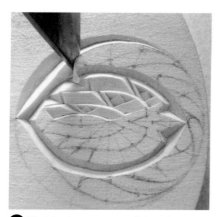

105 Finish the carving of the chip with a cut that follows the shape of the dewdrop.

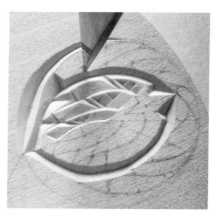

106 Make a straight cut at the top of the second petal at an angle of about 60 degrees.

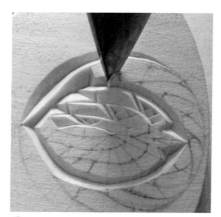

107 Finish the carving of the chip with the second cut.

Without removing the knife from the wood, lead the knife to the outside edge of the pattern **108**.

Now change the grip of the knife in your hand and undercut the second facet of the contour line carving **109**. Repeat these steps for the remaining petals in this section of the pattern.

Next, make a cut at an angle of about 90 degrees where the last shape in the section overlaps the shape in the next section **110**. Lay the knife close to the wood surface and undercut it 2-3mm from the cut **111**. Then redraw those lines that were removed while undercutting **112**.

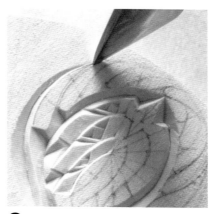

108 Lead the knife to the edge of the pattern while undercutting the first facet of the contour line carving.

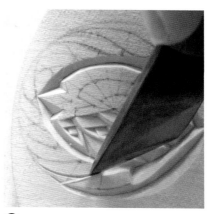

109 Finish carving the second facet of the chip.

110 Make a cut at an angle of about 90 degrees where the first shape overlaps the second one.

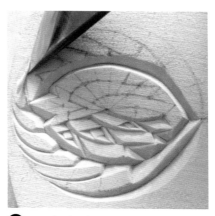

111 Lay the knife close to the wood surface and undercut the wood 2–3mm from the cut.

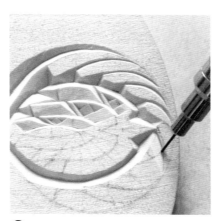

112 Redraw the lines that were removed while undercutting.

Next, carve the six-sided chip at the base. First, undercut the short base side at an angle of about 60 degrees 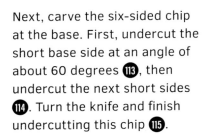, then undercut the next short sides **114**. Turn the knife and finish undercutting this chip **115**.

Undercut the top two sides of the rhombus, which is also at the base of the pattern, at an angle of about 90 degrees **116**. Then undercut the top of the rhombus like a straight-wall chip **117**. Make a cut inside the rhombus from one point to another **118**.

113 Undercut the short base sides of the six-sided chip at the base of the central pattern.

114 Undercut two more short sides of the six-sided chip.

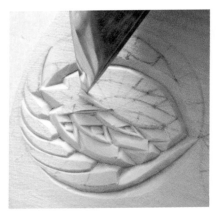

115 Finish carving the six-sided chip.

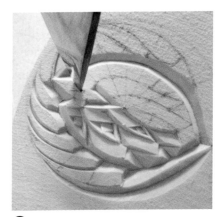

116 Undercut the top two sides of the rhombus at an angle of about 90 degrees.

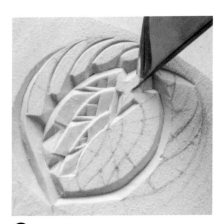

117 Carve the top of the rhombus.

118 Make a cut inside the rhombus.

Now finish the rhombus by making two undercuts .

Continue the short side of the six-sided chip with a cut ⑫⓿, and then make a second undercut, completing the carving of this contour line.

The final stage in the pattern is the carving of triangles, or stars, on the outside edge of the two-sided chips at the perimeter of the pattern. Draw small equilateral triangles in random order ⑫①. Then carve them at an angle of about 60 degrees ⑫②.

The right side of the pattern has been carved ⑫③. Repeat these steps to finish carving the second half of the pattern.

The carving is now complete ⑫④.

119 Make two undercuts to finish the carving of the rhombus.

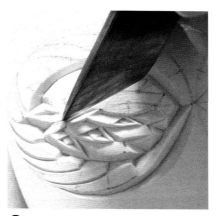

120 Make a short cut next to the six-sided chip.

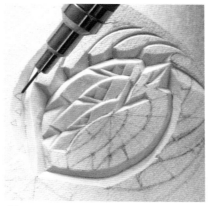

121 Draw small equilateral triangles on the outside edge of the two-sided chips at the perimeter of the pattern.

122 Carve the triangles at an angle of about 60 degrees.

123 The right side of the pattern is now complete.

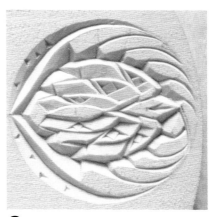

124 The carving of the whole pattern is now complete.

TEMPLATES

TEMPLATE SIZES
All templates are shown at 100% size. See page 12
for how to transfer them to your basswood board.

PATTERN 1

PATTERN 2

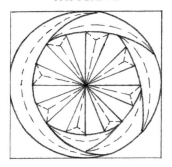

PATTERN 3

PATTERN 4

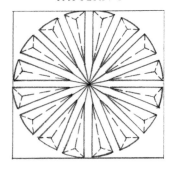

PATTERN 5

PATTERN 6

PATTERN 7

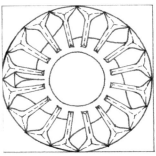

PATTERN 8

PATTERN 9

PATTERN 10

PATTERN 11

PATTERN 12

PATTERN 13

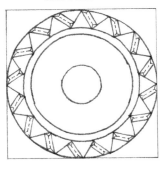

PATTERN 14

PATTERN 15

INDEX

ABOUT THE AUTHOR

Tatiana Baldina is a professional woodcarving artist who lives and works in Russia. She specializes in chip carving and chose to study the subject as part of her Applied Fine Arts degree at the Volga Regional State University. After graduating, Tatiana went on to create many of her own original pieces; she also worked for several companies producing carved boxes and other items for the home. Tatiana is a Laureate of The International Association of the Creative Professions, Vatikam, France. She has worked as a freelance woodcarver since 2014.

Follow on Instagram: @tatbalcarvings
Show us your chip carving using the hashtag #chipcarving

First published 2023 by
Guild of Master Craftsman Publications Ltd
Castle Place, 166 High Street, Lewes, East Sussex, BN7 1XU, UK

Text © Tatiana Baldina, 2023

Copyright in the Work © GMC Publications Ltd, 2023

ISBN 978-1-78494-662-3

A catalogue record for this book is available from the British Library.

Publisher Jonathan Bailey
Production Director Jim Bulley
Senior Project Editor Tom Kitch
Managing Art Editor Robin Shields
Editor Theresa Bebbington
Designer Ginny Zeal
Main photography Andrew Perris
Step-by-step photography Tatiana Baldina

Colour origination by GMC Reprographics
Printed and bound in China

To place an order, contact:
GMC Publications Ltd, Castle Place, 166 High Street,
Lewes, East Sussex, BN7 1XU, United Kingdom
Tel: +44 (0)1273 488005
www.gmcbooks.com